DISCARD

D1409482

DISCARD

PRAISE FOR ROB SALAFIA
AND *LEADING FROM YOUR BEST SELF*

A masterful contribution to the landscape of leadership development, as well as a practical, hands-on manual for personal and professional growth—as seen through the eyes of a consummate performing artist and executive coach. A compelling read that will leave you wanting more.

—**Marshall Goldsmith, author of the #1** *New York Times* **bestseller** *Triggers*

Leading from Your Best Self is an incredible playbook for developing executive presence and influence. Rob is a consummate storyteller and relies on his background in the performing arts to teach us numerous techniques like "landing" and "expanding." Great lessons that will immediately make you a more effective leader.

—**Kevin Kruse, CEO, LEADx.Org**

The majority of books on executive presence say, "Here's what I think works for most people. . . ." Rob Salafia's says, "Let's find out what will work for you." *Leading from Your Best Self* is a customized development plan for becoming the best version of you as a leader.

—**Paul Smith, author of the bestselling books** *Lead with a Story* **and** *Sell with a Story*

In his new book, Rob will show you how to discover, appreciate, and take your Best Self with you. He reveals the secrets to building a powerful executive presence by tapping into your natural strengths and gifts. He will also guide you on how to sustain these behaviors in your daily work lives.

—**Anne Molignano, SVP, Head of Human Resources NA, Sony Music Entertainment**

Any rising leader who works with Rob is in great hands, and now this book gives you Rob's wisdom and coaching, and your full potential, at your fingertips.

—**Joshua Margolis, Professor of Business Administration, Harvard Business School**

Rob's central messages are a priceless guide to the art of truly connecting with others. Though compelling stories and courageous examples, Rob gives us guideposts to living—and leading—with greater authenticity and purpose.

Leaders at all levels can benefit from these clear and straightforward tips for enhancing your impact, starting from the core of who you are as a person.

—**Julie Staudenmier, Vice President, Talent**
Management and Development Pfizer, Inc.

If it's true—as Shakespeare famously wrote—that "all the world's a stage," then Rob Salafia, through his brilliant and captivating new leadership book, *Leading from Your Best Self*, has come along to help us take center stage ... and to shine. A masterful storyteller, Rob draws on his unique background in the performing arts, while sharing many powerful lessons from his own personal leadership journey, to captivate and entertain the reader from start to finish. In so doing, we are instructed on, and inspired to, uncover and explore our own stories ... leading us each to discover our own very best selves.

—**Todd Cherches, CEO of BigBlueGumball, Adjunct**
Professor of leadership at New York University, and
Lecturer on leadership at Columbia University

With a wealth of experience in both theater performance and corporate learning, Rob Salafia brings a perspective few executive coaches can match. In *Leading from Your Best Self*, he has developed a blueprint for success from which leaders at all levels—regardless of field—can benefit. Follow his advice, and you'll not only grow as a leader, but you'll also excel at creating environments in which everyone around you can do the same.

—**Steve Curtis, Vice President, Olympic Marketing,**
Toyota North America

As my coach, Rob motivated me to work hard and guided me to develop the skills necessary to deliver an engaging and relevant presentation to 500 credit risk officers. His dedication to my development and his ability to challenge at just the right time enabled me to bring my story to life.

In his book, *Leading from Your Best Self*, Rob merges his deep experience working with leaders at all levels with a solid background in theater and the performing arts. By using the tools provided in this book, you will be better equipped to step into any new situation with poise and confidence.

—**Darryl Fess, President, Brookline Bank, Boston, MA**

In his book, *Leading from Your Best Self*, Rob Salafia delivers authentic stories with a twinkle in his eye that makes them unforgettable. For me, this book provides an easy reference guide of reminders on how to make every connection personal and enduring, both onstage and through the camera lens.

—**Steve Aveson, News Anchor, KRON4 TV,**
San Francisco

If you have ever received feedback that you need to improve your executive presence, but no one was able to tell you how, this is the book for you. Rob describes in vivid detail a full range of capabilities and skills necessary to stand tall, find your authentic voice, and deliver your message with impact.

—**Mike Figliuolo, Managing Director of *thought*** **LEADERS, LLC and author of *One Piece of Paper*,** ***Lead Inside the Box*, and *The Elegant Pitch***

Rob Salafia is an authority on executive presence and influence. In his book, he shows us that "being present is both a choice and a necessity." You will learn highly-effective, easy-to-remember techniques that will help you become an authentic and confident leader. A must read for those who want to have an impact.

—**Will G. Foussier, CEO and cofounder @Ace-Up, Inc.** **Cambridge, MA**

In an incredibly rich field book for personal and leadership development, *Leading from Your Best Self* is both hugely practical and enjoyable. Rob's first act as a performing artist enables him to bring a unique perspective to the "art" of personal growth. Highly recommended.

—**Jean Gomes, coauthor of the *New York Times*** **bestseller, *The Way We're Working Isn't Working***

We are living in a time where so many people feel like impostors at work. Their work persona has separated from who they really are. This book provides a way for us to see ourselves as others see us and use that knowledge to hone the leadership skills that are so elusive in our organizations. It is time well spent to read, practice, and share Rob's story to be your best.

—**Anne M. Hunnex, MS, Organizational** **Change Consultant**

In the world of business, the ability to connect and create followership for your ideas is what distinguishes leaders from managers. To do this effectively, one needs to look inside of oneself and start to understand that "you are your message." I had the privilege to work with Rob for a number of years and behind his humble yet strong appearance, is someone who is a master at unlocking the potential in others—this book is a strong testament of the valuable work that he delivers and comes highly recommended!

—**Alex Klein, Sr. Director, Talent & Organizational**
Effectiveness, Lumileds

Some books change us. Their powerful, personal messages move us to discover an entirely new potential within ourselves. Rob's book is one of those. His masterful storytelling and fun, easy-to-read way of sharing insights, advice, and tips for improving one's leadership presence and communication effectiveness make for delightful and near-instant personal growth. Every leader . . . every person . . . will benefit from Rob's messages and wisdom.

—**Dave Kruczlincki, President, High Peaks Strategic**
Business Advisors

We all have a story. Some of us are better at sharing it than others. Rob is no ordinary executive coach. Most coaches follow some script—and most insightful leaders have heard the script before, provoking some short-term inquisition, at best. Rob finds a way to have you ask yourself the most difficult yet basic questions—the questions that can define every leader. Rob gets to the heart of what makes us tick, of what defines us, and what we are most passionate about.

Leading from Your Best Self is not about Rob—it is about you. It is about what is within you, and how you turn your experiences, your passions, your own stories into your Best Self.

—**Kosta Ligris, Esq., CEO, Ligris**
Entrepreneur, Philanthropist, Storyteller

Leading from Your Best Self is a PAGE TURNER—and once you start reading this incredible book—you will NOT be able to put it down. Rob Salafia's unique leadership methodology offers not only sage advice—but a step-by-step recipe for any leader to traverse from where they are now to where they NEED to be.

—**Bobby Maher, former CEO, St. Christopher's,**
Dobby Ferry, NY

Rob has opened my eyes to things of which I was totally oblivious. His reverse career path, from a traveling theater and tap-dancing artist to a businessman, has given him wisdom that we can all gain from.

We know Presence when we see it in someone but we can't quite always pin it down. Rob explains it: As in theater, Presence is about how you enter and how you exit, how you land and how you free the limits of your breath. How you listen with your eyes! How you engage an audience by making every cell in your body speak out with you.

Leading from Your Best Self will be a manual and a friend. It shares the wisdom of a traveling performer who was a keen observer of himself and others, who connected with his audience through breath, and who spoke not to talk but to be heard. The book speaks intimately to our internal silence and wisdom and calls it out to be our partner in life and in performance on our life's stage.

—John Prot, CEO, Stromasys

In *Leading from Your Best Self*, Rob Salafia, brings the reader to the reality that most leadership books skim over; that the fabric of who we are, what we experience and the stories we hold dear can help us become the leader we want to be, or rather, have had inside us all along. Through insightful exercises and questions, each chapter brings you closer to the leader you are capable of being. This is the book I've been looking for, and I am so excited to put it into action—with my best self forward.

—Donna Scarola, Sr. Manager, Global Performance
& Development, Johnson & Johnson

"Poetry" said Novalis, the 18th-century German philosopher, "heals the wounds inflicted by reason." Paraphrasing Novalis, today we need the arts in order to activate our deep human creativity to heal the wounds inflicted by our old leadership and management paradigm. Rob's book is a key contribution to the new leadership that is called for today. He speaks from his personal experience and highlights many of the new principles and practices. Highly recommended.

—Otto Scharmer, founder of MITx u.lab and author
of *The Essentials of Theory U* (Berrett-Koehler, 2018)

Rob's knowledge of business and theater enables him to coach, energize, and challenge a room of senior executives. He shares his insights with you in this book, making it the next best thing to having your own personal executive coach.

—**Gloria Schuck, EdM & EdD, Harvard**
Lecturer, MIT (from the Foreword)

I was at the Silver Bay leadership conference that Rob speaks about in Chapter 1. What was extraordinary was watching Hope become herself, as Rob says "her best self" right in front of us. Rob has a gift for bringing out the strength within people and helping them use it and access it in times of challenge. In that way he exemplifies one of the core principles of coaching: leveraging the strength of the coachee and helping them shine their light on the world.

—**Erica Schwartz, Leadership Coach**

There is an art and science to leading. There are countless authors who can write about one or the other. I can think of no one better qualified than Rob Salafia to share the secrets of both the Art & the Science of how "showing up"—fully and powerfully—maximizes our potential. I have worked with Rob for decades in countless programs where our common goal is to help participants gain greater clarity (self-awareness) and comfort (self-acceptance) with who they are. If you want to learn how to become more of who you are, who you are meant to be, this is the book for you!

—**Scott Snook, Senior Lecturer of Business**
Administration, Harvard Business School.

Rob Salafia, a master alchemist in the art of leadership transformation, joyously translates the laudable premise of *Leading from Your Best Self*, from aspiration to practice.

In this fine book, steeped in story, lessons drawn from a life in the theater and decades of teaching leadership presence, you will find inspiration and skillful means for developing the art and cultivating the lifelong craft of discovering how you can lead from your own best self. Rob's book is a bar-raising gift to the field, but more importantly, it will help you hone what's best in you and share it vividly with the world.

—**Marc Zegans, Creative Development Advisor**

LEADING FROM YOUR
BEST
SELF

Develop Executive Poise,
Presence, and Influence to
Maximize Your Potential

ROB SALAFIA

NEW YORK   CHICAGO   SAN FRANCISCO
ATHENS   LONDON   MADRID
MEXICO CITY   MILAN   NEW DELHI
SINGAPORE   SYDNEY   TORONTO

Copyright © 2019 by Rob Salafia. All rights reserved. Printed in the United States of America. Except as permitted under the United States Copyright Act of 1976, no part of this publication may be reproduced or distributed in any form or by any means, or stored in a database or retrieval system, without the prior written permission of the publisher.

1 2 3 4 5 6 7 8 9   QVS   23 22 21 20 19 18

ISBN 978-1-260-13217-5
MHID   1-260-13217-X

e-ISBN 978-1-260-13218-2
e-MHID   1-260-13218-8

Design by Lee Fukui and Mauna Eichner

Library of Congress Cataloging-in-Publication Data

Names: Salafia, Rob, author.
Title: Leading from your best self: develop executive poise, presence, and
   influence to maximize your potential / Rob Salafia.
Description: 1 Edition. | New York : McGraw-Hill Education, 2018.
Identifiers: LCCN 2018030691| ISBN 9781260132175 (hardback) | ISBN 126013217X (ebook)
Subjects: LCSH: Leadership. | Executive ability. | BISAC: BUSINESS &
   ECONOMICS / Leadership.
Classification: LCC HD57.7 .S2395 2018 | DDC 658.4/092—dc23 LC record available at
https://lccn.loc.gov/2018030691

McGraw-Hill Education products are available at special quantity discounts to use as premiums and sales promotions or for use in corporate training programs. To contact a representative, please visit the Contact Us pages at www.mhprofessional.com.

To my wife, Pamela, and my daughter, Maya,
with whom I live a most miraculous story.

CONTENTS

CONTENTS

FOREWORD

Leading from Your Best Self is an aspiration for all of us. It's probably why you are drawn to this book. Rob took his career in acting and performing arts, combined it with leadership development and executive coaching, and "Voila!" he created *Leading from Your Best Self* to help you increase your poise, presence, and influence.

For almost 40 years I've coached executives and taught graduate students at the Massachusetts Institute of Technology, and I have taught leadership for the past 15 years. In the decade I've known Rob I've worked with him in both consulting and academic settings. Every year I invite Rob to teach a class in my leadership course. He is both masterful and insightful, prompting impressive responses from my students after only one 90-minute class! Responses such as:

- "When I used the techniques that Rob taught us I was not pretending to be someone else. I was instead presenting more of me. That's part of leadership presence."
- "It was a very transformative experience where I learned about the importance of developing personal presence, compelling storytelling, and ways of connecting authentically with others."

People are hungry to become better leaders. A CEO and I have been working to design and deliver a leadership program for members of her organization. In speaking to people regarding the skills they need, "executive presence and voice are at the top of the list"! Rob and *Leading from Your Best Self* will form an important part of that program.

The foundation of leadership is self-awareness, and requires inquiry, reflection, and feedback. Rob provides you with tools and guides you with reflective questions and exercises in every chapter, along with references to articles and videos to deepen your understanding and demonstrate the practice, such as the *Breathe-Connect-Land* Exercise in Chapter 2 and the *Present and Open* Exercise in Chapter 5. Rob has also designed a reflection process to examine your Best Self Moments.

Rob's knowledge of business and theater enables him to coach, energize, and challenge a room of senior executives. He shares his insights with you in this book, making it the next best thing to having your own personal executive coach.

Leadership requires lifelong, self-directed learning. As a CEO guest in my leadership class said, "The person who cares most about your development is you. You have to drive it."

I invite you to take advantage of all the learning opportunities in *Leading from Your Best Self*. Read it carefully and work through the exercises Rob provides. You will be glad you did!

Gloria Schuck, EdM, EdD, Harvard
Lecturer, MIT
Watertown, Massachusetts

PREFACE

If you are reading this book, the concept of being your Best Self and the topic of executive presence has caught your attention and interest. Maybe . . .

- You have been passed up for a promotion—even though you are clearly smart enough and technically competent. *No one can put a finger on exactly what the issue is, but it's enough to hold you back.*
- You're a manager and someone on your team has the potential to shine but is struggling to *find his or her voice.* You are looking for a way to initiate a deeper conversation.
- You have a burning desire to make a difference. It's not about the money any longer. *You are seeking guidance and an inspirational spark.*

If you identify with any of these statements, you're in luck. This book is designed to help you recognize, develop, and channel your most natural and gifted parts of yourself into your work and personal life.

WHY IS DEVELOPING EXECUTIVE POISE AND PRESENCE IMPORTANT?

It's simple. Externally, we are evaluated by how well we show up and navigate the work environment and culture. Those in charge of making promotion decisions need to confidently answer questions such as "Do we see this person as promotable?" "Do others listen to his or her ideas?" and "Will this person be a good fit on the team and able to influence the decision-making process?"

More important, however, are the intrinsic motivations and deep-seated needs we have to live an authentic life. By cultivating executive presence, we not only improve how others experience us, but enhance our capacity to lead a life that moves us toward the ends of our own choosing.

HOW TO READ THIS BOOK

The ideas in this book will help you think more deeply about how you show up as a person, how you engage others, and how you lead. The chapters can be read independently given the area that is most relevant to you or from front to back. The examples and stories presented draw from my own experiences in theater as a performing artist, as well as in business as an executive coach. You will find that the challenges are universal and relatable.

AN AERIAL VIEW

Let's take a quick look at what is contained in the book chapter by chapter.

Introduction

"Rooted in the Theater and Performing Arts"

This is an open letter to you, the reader, that offers a few reference points regarding my journey as a performing artist—and why and how integrating methods from the performing arts can help you learn to lead from your Best Self.

"On Becoming a Natural"

In this section I share a road map for mastery that artists have taken for centuries called the apprentice model. The apprentice model is built on the premise that personal development in any area of expertise comes in stages and relies on good coaching, a system for learning, and a platform for failure. This model can be helpful to consider as you begin your own personal development process.

Chapter 1: The Art of Being Extraordinary

We begin by introducing the concept of the Best Self in the field of positive psychology. The idea is that every person has the capacity to be extraordinary by appreciating and nurturing his or her best qualities and gifts. Specific case examples are used to bring the concept to life. You will learn to identify your keys to being extraordinary. Core concepts include *Trials by Fire*, *Signature Stance*, and *Playing to Be Heard*.

Chapter 2: The Art of Landing

In this chapter we'll discuss the notion of "landing" as the foundation for building executive poise, presence, and leadership agility. Landing means more than just putting on a game face. It is a quality of graciousness and responsiveness that puts others at ease while still able to make decisions under immense pressure and constant change. The ideas we'll explore in this chapter include landing in the present moment, exploring the signals of presence, and developing an authentic persona.

Chapter 3: The Art of Expanding

In this chapter we will explore the notion of expanding into experience as the choice to feel large, finding one's authentic voice, and being one's Best Self. This includes the ability to create a space that allows others to bring their Best Self forward as well.

Chapter 4: The Art of Expanding into Conflict

In this chapter we will explore the more advanced challenge that we all face, the notion of extending our poise and presence into zones of conflict. The more we learn how to not only navigate through it, but actually expand into conflict, the more we realize the tremendous payoff in terms of honing reputation, building trust, reducing risk, and improving business results.

Chapter 5: The Art of Developing Physical and Vocal Presence

In this chapter, we will build awareness around the messages that we send through our facial and physical gestures. We will learn how to cultivate a resting smile, how to be present and open, and how to fix the leaks to our personal power. We will explore how these skills are applicable in both our day-to-day interactions and presentations.

Chapter 6: The Art of Transitioning

In this chapter we are going to look at two of the most important types of transitions:

1. The smaller transitions that we make in our day-to-day interactions and activities.
2. The larger transitions that we make in our careers.

In theater, as in real life, transitions can be the focal point of anxiety and drama. Paying attention to them is critical if we are to be successful in both our day-to-day interactions and navigating the trajectory of our lives.

Chapter 7: The Art of Self-Discovery and Authenticity

In this chapter, we will explore the concept of authenticity. We will introduce a process of self-discovery as the path toward creating a solid foundation for one's own authentic leadership.

Chapter 8: The Art of Relating and Connecting

In this chapter we will explore the different levels on which we relate to others and how these levels either block or facilitate great results. We will discuss the foundations of trust and the secrets to connecting authentically with others. At the end of the chapter we will explore the notion of multiple identities and insights toward living an integrated life.

Chapter 9: The Art of Story Sharing, Storytelling, and Meaning Making

In this chapter, we will look at the power of story as an essential tool of the transformational leader. We will distinguish the difference between story sharing and storytelling. We will look at what it means to step into the role of the leader of culture and to create meaning. In addition, we will explore what makes a great story, as well as what it takes to become a great storyteller.

Chapter 10: The Art of Influencing

This chapter will help you understand the sources of influence and power within organizations. Our focus will remain on the development of personal power as the most sustainable way for leaders to create meaningful action. We will explore key communication tools to open others to your ideas and guide action. We will also learn how to use the power of intention to galvanize your expressive capabilities and maximize the impact of your messages.

Chapter 11: The Art of Leading Change

In this chapter, I will share several real-life examples of how leaders have put metaphors, stories, and various narrative frameworks to use in leading change.

Chapter 12: The Art of Making Great Presentations

In this chapter, I will share with you one of my most memorable moments in front of an audience, as well as some of my favorite coaching engagements with individuals on highly visible and critical presentations. From these stories, I will identify a few key principles and practices in both preparation and delivery that you can take away and put into action immediately.

Chapter 13: The Art of Creating a Learning Organization

In this final chapter, I offer the metaphor of an ensemble theater company as an inspirational model for creating a learning organization. The characteristics and traits of theater ensembles suggest new ways of considering what learning means for the individual, team, and organization. I will also offer a variety of tools that can be employed to foster a culture of learning within your team and organization.

ACKNOWLEDGMENTS

I would like to begin by acknowledging Fred Green for being the catalyst for this book. He graciously introduced me to my literary agent, Ken Lizotte. Ken recognized the value of my story, deftly guided me through the proposal process, and delivered on his promise. Ken, you have been a consistent support; however, I am still waiting for that champagne toast. The call with Cheryl Ringer at McGraw-Hill was a stunner. Right away she told me that being a tap dancer in NYC she deeply resonated with the concept of the book. Thank you for appreciating my vision and making this book a reality.

My editing team was second to none. Cheryl Ringer for her rigorous guidance. Elena Petricone for being my consistent and trusted partner throughout the entire process. My wife, Pamela Rice, for adding her laser eye, creativity, and astute mind to the editing of key chapters. And an extra special callout to Marc Zegans for generously sharing his inspired, authentic, and brilliant insights to every inch of this book. Marc, you appeared at just the right time and went right to the heart of the matter!

Gloria Schuck for her belief in my work. You get me.

Debbi Bromley for inviting me to collaborate on her powerful research study focused on the use of a theater-based approach to develop storytelling skills.

Bobby Maher for being a champion of my work and this book.

Mike Figliuolo and Michael Robbins for their support and guidance.

Deborah Ancona for opening the door to becoming a member of the MIT Leadership Center Executive Coaching team. I have learned so much from my MIT colleagues as well as my coaching clients in these programs. It has been a mutually beneficial growth experience and gave me a solid foundation for this book.

To all my coaching clients from whom many of the stories in this book are based. To all of those who have paved the way, opened doors, invited collaboration, and inspired me to find my own unique voice.

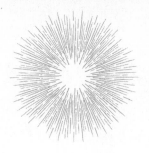

INTRODUCTION

"ROOTED IN THE THEATER AND PERFORMING ARTS"

In his work on social cognitive theory, psychologist Albert Bandura asserts that theater is a powerful way to build self-efficacy, or a belief in one's ability to accomplish a task or succeed in specific situations. In the world of business, this is called self-confidence, and it is critical for career success. In this book, I will bring to life many lessons that I have learned as a theater professional turned executive coach and show you how you can apply these lessons in your roles at work and in life.

Act I

For the first half of my career I was a performing artist traveling much of North America delivering a unique, one-person variety show. Storytelling was always at the heart of my work, and I was fully captivated with this artform in 1977 while attending the National Association for the Preservation and Perpetuation of Storytelling Conference in Jonesboro, Tennessee. I was enthralled by the power of these amazing performers who could capture the imagination of their audience and create lasting and vivid images in their audience's minds. My first and fondest memory at the festival is of Doc McConnell standing in front of his medicine truck pitching old-time snake oil and telling tales as tall as a field of cornstalks (Figure I.1). You just got lost in his stories.

1

FIGURE I.1 Doc McConnell and his Old-Time Medicine Show

Dance, mime, and circus were also areas of interest and specialty. The image of me in Figure I.2 was taken during the main stage performance at the Edmonton Street Performers Festival. The image in Figure I.3 was taken in 1979 during my first year as a performer.

I studied the art of tap dance with renowned dancers including Gregory Hines, Leon Collins, Steve Condos, Jimmy Slyde, and many other legends from New York City, Los Angeles, Boston, and Philadelphia. And, in 1989, I was awarded a residency with the celebrated tap dancer Honi Coles. Theirs was a culture of excellence, self-determination, and courage. One of my most memorable moments was in the early eighties, taking a cab with some friends to Smalls Paradise, a nightclub on 125th Street in Harlem, and being invited by the late Buster Brown to dance in front of a 16-piece jazz orchestra. Smalls Paradise was second only to the Cotton Club in its heyday. It was unforgettable.

I also became a wire walker (Think Philippe Petit, who walked across the World Trade Towers ... only not that high!) and learned to challenge and conquer my fear of heights.

The Road Less Taken

My journey into performing started in 1978. I was fresh out of college and had just begun to explore the world of theater and performing rather than pursuing a career in political geography. That winter I had learned to juggle and started to do a bit of performing in front of small audiences.

I wanted to learn more and found out about a gifted teacher, Tony Montanaro, who held summer classes in Maine for professional performers. I enrolled

FIGURE I.2 Rob, tap dancing at the 1990 Edmonton Street
Performers Festival, Edmonton, Alberta

FIGURE I.3 Rob, Street Clown, Faneuil Hall, Boston, MA 1979

in his three-month mime and storytelling workshop. This was a huge commitment, and I was eager to prove myself.

One morning I stood facing a wall in the large red barn where we had our classes, juggling three Indian clubs. These were crude, homemade instruments, heavy and a bit unwieldy. I was quite proud of the fact that I could handle more than just three juggling balls and hacked away at trying to perfect a few basic moves with the clubs.

Without any announcement, Tony entered the barn and started to walk past me, when he stopped, looked at me, and made a comment: "Salafia," he said, "you just don't look like a juggler." And then walked away.

Maybe I was just trying to get his attention, but when he said these words I was shocked at first, then dismayed, and eventually thrilled that he had actually noticed me. His comment has stayed with me to this day. It didn't matter that I was capable with the Indian clubs—or at least, not as much as I'd hoped. Tony still didn't *see* me as a juggler. His comment captured an important part of my initial training, and, at the time, got me to realize that I had some work to do. Looking back, I now realize that with this simple comment Tony opened a door to self-discovery. He got me to start thinking about what I wanted and inspired me to create a vision for myself as an artist.

· · ·

When was the last time you received feedback about your presence? Was it specific and actionable—or was it vague, like Tony's? How did you react? Did you get defensive? Did it shock you? Did it make you want to dig in deeper?

As an artist, I was determined to find my way in this new world of performing. There was an inner drive that kept me coming back for more. I sought out various teachers, joined a tap dance company, became a street performer, developed a theater show, acquired new skills, failed often, learned a lot, and developed my own unique style. It was one continual learning process, and when I look back upon my time in the theater, there are many lessons that I draw upon daily:

- Be a learning machine.
- Cultivate patience.
- Practice humility.
- Do what you love.
- Take all your experience with you.

- Forgive yourself.
- Simplify.
- Let the audience in.
- Be vulnerable.
- Be the best version of yourself—every day.

Act 2

Today, I am a speaker and facilitator of experiential learning programs, as well as an executive coach within the Massachusetts Institute of Technology's mid-career MBA programs. I have had the honor of working with a diverse and stellar group of global leaders. At MIT, a person comes to the experience wanting *something*. Sometimes it is a clear goal, for others it is less known.

Some say they are looking to sharpen their technical skill set. For others, it is deeper. For most, it is a pause point in their career and the beginning of a personal transformation. My job is to listen and look for clues to figure out where they might be on their journey of personal development so I can give them the right nudge.

I invite you to think of this book as a gentle nudge to pause and reflect on your own development. Let's first begin by setting the stage for learning,

ON BECOMING A NATURAL

When we meet people who show up with a natural and confident presence, we assume that they were born that way. In truth, some are. Most, however, have learned that it takes training, preparation, and experimentation to achieve this level of confidence.

I am always amazed at the amount of time executives typically spend organizing and creating the perfect PowerPoint deck for their strategic communication, presentation, or pitch. They will go to great lengths to create charts that are packed with data—so much so that the slides are impossible to read without a magnifying glass from a close distance, let alone from the tenth row. Then, such executives put all of their materials into their briefcase and vow to practice the rest of their presentation in the cab ride on the way to the conference. How do you think that will turn out?

For the actor or well-trained performer, our approach is the inverse. We learn that it is the nuance of *how* we say what we say that makes the difference.

We learn that to appear natural in front of others, and for our messages to land well, it takes discipline and practice. We focus on developing our minds, hearts, and bodies. We learn to develop vocal and physical flexibility and range. We learn to prepare for our parts, inhabit our roles, land on stage, hit our marks, and deliver our lines. We learn how to relax inside of ourselves, get focused, and connect authentically with our fellow actors and our audience. We learn that being present is both a choice and a necessity.

If you imagine a circus acrobat, you'll likely picture someone who has bright energy, a strong and flexible physique, and clear focus. Acrobats are immediately recognizable. They send the message, "I am here to dazzle you!" And they send it without saying a word!

Think back to the "naturals" you've worked with in your life. How did they send the message of "leader" without saying a word?

The great performers I've known have several things in common:

- They have love and passion for what they do!
- They have a learning mindset and know how to be coached.
- They know the value of practice and create a system for learning.
- Their preparation is impeccable.
- They know how to reach an audience and understand the impact that they have on that audience.
- They are committed to bringing their Best Self to each and every performance.
- They never take a performance for granted.

Develop a System for Learning

Many performers follow a well-worn path to learning their craft by apprenticing with a master. The apprentice model of learning involves four stages:

1. Novice
2. Apprentice
3. Journeyman
4. Master

Everyone enters as a novice. A novice is someone who has shown an initial talent in an artform and is looking for a way to get started. This is the most precarious part of the journey, and it's also when most people drop out or give up. They put their toe in the water but for some reason do not stay. In this phase it is critical to have the right encouragement and support, to make it fun, and to experience a small taste of success. It is also critical to have a goal and to get through this phase as quickly as possible.

Let me tell you what I mean. In the mid-eighties I was a working performer in the Boston area. I heard about a musical built around a circus theme that was being locally written and produced. I was successful in getting an audition.

To my surprise and delight I was called back to speak to the director and was cast as the lead in the show. The director, Bill Finlay, a former circus wire walker and now chair of the Theater Department at Union College in upstate New York, enticed me with an offer. He said that he had always wanted to put a wire act in a musical, and that if I was willing to learn, he would find a way to incorporate it in the show. I was immediately hooked and took him up on his offer to teach me.

At the time I was living in a loft in Boston. The loft had two large support posts, which were perfect to attach a low steel wire between. I quickly assembled my wire between the two posts about two feet above the floor and spent as much time as possible on it.

In the morning I ate my bowl of cereal on the wire. I read books on it. I even learned how to lie down and relax on it. As a novice, my time on the wire was focused on finding my balance and addressing my fear of falling. Once I became more comfortable and began to learn more complex techniques, I quickly moved from a novice to an apprentice.

Develop a Platform for Failure

The apprentice stage is when one understands the basics but needs guidance. You still need to go to class. You can't really perfect what you're doing without the help of a coach. The teacher reveals to you the nuances of your craft while you build upon your experience and your vocabulary.

I learned to be fully alert and cautious when stepping onto and off of the wire, as these were where most accidents happened. I learned how to breathe through the wire and into the ground to find my balance, where to rest my eyes, and how to change direction.

After about six months of apprenticeship, I felt confident enough to incorporate the skill into my professional act. I entered the third stage of the apprentice model and was now a journeyman wire walker. At this stage it was all about experimentation in front of audiences. Trial and error. Learning the nuances of the art form. This is one of the benefits of being a street performer. It was the most accessible place where I could experiment, fail, learn, and grow.

It Takes an Outside Eye

Much of my street performing experience took place at Faneuil Hall Marketplace in Boston, as well as at city festivals across the United States and Canada. My show was a blend of physical theater, slapstick, tap dance, and audience participation.

I had just created a new rope balancing routine and began to employ it at the beginning of my show; typically, I started with the less-practiced routines and built up to the stronger and more impressive ones.

My act was solid, but a fellow performer challenged my thinking. He confirmed that the new routine was working great but said it seemed wasted at the beginning of my act. He also said that my audience participation routine at the end was unique, fun, and effective, but something was missing. "What if you blended the two together?" he asked.

And there it was. He was able to see something that elevated my good performance to an outstanding one.

The point is this: I had developed the discipline of practice and a mindset for continual improvement, and I was open to direction. My colleague was not so much telling me what to do but saw an opportunity to create an optimal experience between me and my audience. I encourage you to read this book with the same mindset for continual improvement. I will not be telling you, the reader, what to do, as much as offering ideas on how you can create your own optimal experience of executive presence.

Letting Go

Toward the end of my time in street performing something remarkable happened.

It is 1990 and I am standing in the middle of a large circle of about 300 people in front of the Faneuil Hall building. The sun is shining bright. The sweet smell of sausage and peppers and the sound of Peruvian flute music fill the air. I bend down to pick up my top hat and am about to start my first routine when I stand up, take a deep breath, and pause. I look around the circle into the faces of the audience and see a sense of anticipation and wonder that comes when something extraordinary is about to happen. I am not in a rush. I am fully in the moment.

In this moment, *I actually "feel" something inside of me drop away*. It was something I had been carrying for many years. The need to be liked. The need to impress. The need "to make something happen." In the past I experienced this as a discomfort that made me rush through the moment. It made me try too hard. I held on to an image of who I wanted to be and acted out of a sense of desperation rather than confidence. I resorted to cajoling my audience rather than enticing them to join me on a journey.

But this moment is different. From my right, a small two-year-old girl begins to walk out and into the middle of the circle. She is dressed like a princess and has a pink balloon tied to her wrist floating just above her head. She wanders out into the space in that oblivious way that kids sometimes do. The whole audience is captivated by her. I know what is happening. It is not about me at all; it is about the moment.

Two things cross my mind. First, to give the child "her" moment, and second, to return her safely to her parents. I find myself slowly walking toward the child. I put my finger to my lips and signal to the audience to be still. While holding the attention of the audience with my eyes, I put one finger under each of her arms and lightly and carefully lift them up high and give a big Ta-da!

The whole audience bursts into applause. It is in this moment that I guide the child back to her parents. I can see the appreciation in the faces of the audience, which creates a very human experience for all.

This is the essence of theater and what we all crave in our day-to-day work experiences. A bit of sensitivity and acknowledgment, the feeling of connection, and relating in a more authentic manner with each other.

Mastery Happens

Mastery is no mystery, and yet it is. It comes after years of repetition and experience. Mastery happens without you even knowing it. It's a state of being. It is when the skills that you have acquired over years are set in your bones. When every fiber of your being is finely tuned to the problem that you need to solve or the experience that you want to create.

BRIDGING THE GAP

In my work in leadership development, I have noticed a gap between the areas of building *skills* and the areas of building *self-awareness*. It was only when I became certified as an executive coach that I began to see a bridge between the two. Building self-awareness asks that we look inside of ourselves. It enables us to see both our strengths and weaknesses, our biases and assumptions, and our purpose. In turn, building skills trains us to develop an experimentation and learning mindset. As we develop and grow we become more self-aware.

For me, accelerated learning comes from this combination of building an inner focus of awareness and an outer focus of skills. One feeds upon the other.

Throughout the book I will present ample opportunities for you to reflect upon your own pivotal experiences and decision points. In addition, I will present to you many skill sets with which you can experiment. If at all possible, I advise you to read the book fully first and then mark those areas that you would like to focus on and develop. While you will find ample information to lead from your Best Self in the pages of this book, I have put together additional resources at www.leadingfromyourbestself.com/resources.

Find someone who will act as a peer coach to go on the journey with you. It is always helpful to have someone who gets you and will keep you energized and focused and hold you accountable for your commitments. You will find satisfaction and insight in doing the same for him or her.

MY INVITATION

Take charge of your own learning. Strive to be the best version of yourself—every day.

So, what are you waiting for?

On with the show!

THE ART OF BEING
EXTRAORDINARY

Courage is the moment when an ordinary person
becomes an extraordinary being.
—BRIAN JACQUES

A s human beings, we are all born with a unique set of natural gifts and talents. Maybe we have a knack for numbers. Maybe we naturally bring people together to collaborate. Maybe we possess a killer sense of humor that puts people at ease. No matter what, it's a wonderful part of human experience to really see someone in his or her element. Finding a way to draw upon our intrinsic gifts and talents can make the difference between having a good career and a great one. Moreover, cultivating our gifts and utilizing them at the right moments and for the right reasons can also deeply enrich our personal lives.

The following introduction from the Center for Positive Organizations at the University of Michigan gives us a framework for the Best Self:

> Each of us can recall our own extraordinary moments—those moments when we felt that our Best Self was brought to light, affirmed by others, and put into practice in the world. These memories are seared into our minds as moments or situations in which we felt alive, true to our deepest selves, and pursuing our full potential as human beings. Over time, we collect these experiences into a portrait of who we are at our personal best . . . whether

implicit or explicit, stable or changing, this portrait serves as an anchor and a beacon, a personal touchstone of who we are and a guide for who we can become.[1]

The portrait described above is called the Reflected Best Self (RBS). I first came upon the concept of the RBS while leading the delivery of theater-based workshops at Harvard Business School. Participants in the leadership programs of which we were a part engaged in a preprogram 360 assessment based on the RBS. Participants gathered vivid descriptions and narratives of themselves at their best from a variety of individuals with whom they interacted on a regular basis. These narratives and stories described how the participants showed up as leaders, how others experienced them, and the impact they had on others.

FOUNDATIONS IN PSYCHOLOGY

Let's take a quick look at the concepts of Best Self and Reflected Best Self (RBS) and where these terms stand in the field of psychology. Humanistic psychologist Carl Rogers believed that humans have one basic motive: to self-actualize or to fulfill one's potential and achieve the highest level of "human-being-ness" possible. Rogers believed that for a person to achieve self-actualization he or she must be in a state of congruence.

A starting point for self-actualization is provided by Manuela Heberle:

> In psychology, the real self and the ideal self are terms used to describe personality domains. The real self is who we actually are. It is how we think, how we feel, look, and act.... The ideal self, on the other hand, is who we want to be. It is an idealized image that we have developed over time, based on what we have learned and experienced. The ideal self could include components of what our parents have taught us, what we admire in others, what our society promotes, and what we think is in our best interest.[2]

Congruence is a state of being when our real self and ideal self are in harmony and in alignment. How do we get there? We begin by understanding that there may be a difference between how we see ourselves (our self-image), how we want others to see us (our ideal self), and how others actually see us (our real self).

The good news is that the Reflected Best Self process allows us to gather the information necessary to form a clear and accurate picture of our Best Self. The Best Self is the most vital part of the real self. It is how we look, feel, and act when we are at our best. It is a validation of our self-image and a worthy ideal to aspire to.

Through this process we develop an understanding of the strengths, talents, qualities, and gifts that we bring to various situations and what others appreciate about us. We learn to appreciate what is remarkable about us and the value that we bring to our roles.

Again, from the Center for Positive Organizations:

> The RBS creates a pathway to becoming extraordinary, in that it involves envisioning the self at one's best, and then acting on this vision to translate the possibilities for the extraordinary into reality.[3]

TAKE YOUR BEST SELF WITH YOU

It was July 2017, and I was attending the Leadership Forum at Silver Bay in upstate New York. Inside a century-old stone meeting hall, I sat at a table having a conversation with Hope, an early-career woman. After completing an exercise, Hope said to me, "The director in my office told me that I need to improve my executive presence."

As she shared this, I noticed her shoulders slump and her voice weaken. She looked at a loss. I acknowledged her feelings and invited her to talk more about it. Hope explained that she really loved her job, but there was a senior manager in her department who was being excessively hard on her. When she was in front of this person, both Hope's posture and her voice would weaken, and she would lose her confidence. She'd been entrusted with an important presentation to the senior team in a couple of weeks and was understandably very concerned.

I paused and asked her to tell me about a time in her life when she felt her best, most alive, and confident. After considering for a moment, a gentle smile came onto her face. She'd played flute in an award-winning high school marching band—a band so good that it consistently won at the Columbus Day Parade in New York City! I asked Hope to show me what she looked like when she got ready to play. Immediately her posture and presence transformed. She sat up tall and confident as she lifted her arms into her playing position. She exuded joy.

Hope wasn't just a talented contributor to the band either. She led the whole flute section and expected excellence from them. She emphasized to her team the importance of staying focused and in sync at all times—even when they were just marching and not playing. If the judges noticed even one person looking away or being out of formation they would deduct a quarter point. This was the margin of winning or losing.

As Hope spoke, I noticed that she was no longer overwhelmed and depressed. Rather, she was energized, hopeful, and confident. We discussed how she could take this rediscovered confidence with her to work. It was a perfect sense memory to guide her behavior under stress and find her way back to her Best Self. Together, we created a plan to take her Best Self to her upcoming and critical presentation in front of the entire senior team.

BEING AT ONE'S BEST

What does it mean to lead from our Best Self?

> While one's strengths (i.e., competencies, talents, values, personality attributes) lie at the core of one's RBS, the RBS portrait also incorporates a characterization of the state of being at one's best. In this state of being, an individual actively employs strengths to create value, actualize one's potential, and fulfill one's sense of purpose, which generates a constructive experience (emotional, cognitive, or behavioral) for oneself and for others.[4]

The description above can sound a little daunting. You might be wondering, "How does one actually recreate this state of being, especially when faced with a difficult work-related situation?" Let's look again at the example I gave above.

Until our conversation, Hope's upcoming presentation was causing her intense anxiety. By recalling a time when she felt at her best, she unplugged from the anxiety and reconnected with a genuine positive self-image.

TRIALS BY FIRE

We discover our Best Self under pressure, through experimentation, and through risk-taking. Our best qualities, traits, and values are forged in the fires of doubt and uncertainty. It happens when we reach down deep and discover parts of ourselves that might have been unknown to us or that we had only a glimpse of before. It is in these times that we surpass our previously held self-image and step into a new version of ourselves.

Think of it like this . . .

If we were to witness the making of a legendary Japanese sword, we would at first see a dull piece of metal being plunged into a blazing fire till it glowed red-hot. The master would take it out and place it on his anvil. He would pound and fold the steel upon itself. He would then plunge the metal into a vat of water to cool it.

As the legends go, this process would be repeated 10,000 times. This process creates a sword with true strength, resilience, and integrity. This sword was forged through Trial by Fire experiences. This was the process that I was guiding Hope through.

HOPE DISCOVERS HER KEYS TO BEING EXTRAORDINARY

As a musician and member of an award-winning marching band, Hope had developed a system for learning and a mindset of excellence. She knew what it meant to perform under pressure. Now it was time for her to step into a leadership moment in front of the senior team. From our coaching conversations, Hope discovered four keys for getting into an optimal state of body, mind, and spirit.

1. **Finding Her Signature Stance.** Through her flute training, Hope was taught to stand tall yet relaxed. Her arms needed to be raised with her hands placed on the flute in a comfortable yet optimal position. This was likely difficult when she was first learning this posture, but through years of practice it became second nature. Then, under the stress of playing in front of audiences she learned how to maintain and utilize the form to bring out her best performance.

   By getting back into this posture and visualizing herself performing, she sent a clear and positive message to herself: a sense memory of confidence. She felt more focused, more engaged, and more physically present. Her body, mind, and spirit were in sync. This was her *Signature Stance*. I saw the changes happen before my eyes, and I experienced her as being natural, confident, and powerful.

2. **Playing to Be Heard.** Hope had expressed that in certain situations at work, she would lose her confidence, and her voice would get weak. However, when she took on her flute-playing posture and visualized herself playing in the band, she noticed that her body relaxed and her breath became stronger. Developing breath control was part of her training as a flutist. She was taught to "*Play to Be Heard.*" When she spoke about *Playing to Be Heard*, the cadence and tone in her voice became stronger, more relaxed, expressive, and clear.

   We discussed how she could more easily access this power in her voice while speaking in front of others. This was her second key to being her Best Self. (In Chapter 2 we will introduce a number of breathing techniques so that you too can master your breath.)

3. **Adopting a Mindset of Excellence.** The third key for Hope was recalling her role as a leader in the band. She held a strong vision of excellence for herself and her fellow flute players. We discussed how she could hold this vision of excellence and lead herself. Could she be her own coach and demand the very best from herself? Could she put into practice the same principles that she had reinforced with her fellow flute players? How could she enlist others in her development and hold herself accountable? Once she discovered the answers to these questions she felt more in control of the presentation.

4. **Finding Her Groove.** The fourth key for Hope appeared when she started humming her favorite song that the band played. This sense of rhythm, tempo, and timing created a fluid state of mind for Hope. In this state she experienced a sense of physical, mental and emotional congruence. She felt the strength and confidence she'd earned from years of training.

· · ·

All told, these elements became her four triggers with which she could recreate a state of positivity, focus, and confidence in the face of the most intimidating of situations. In other words, these were her keys to being extraordinary.

Hope said that she took these four elements and shared them with a couple of senior leaders in her department. These were folks who supported and wanted the best for her. She practiced her presentation in front of them and received their feedback and encouragement. She also practiced her four keys to being extraordinary with them. They reminded her to stand tall, play to be heard, and find her groove.

When I spoke with Hope after her presentation, she was elated. She said that she felt calm and confident before her presentation. She took control of the moment, stood tall, and spoke in a strong and confident voice. She experienced a deep sense of satisfaction from the experience. Even the senior person who'd been tough on her approached her afterward and congratulated her on a great job.

DISCOVERING YOUR KEYS TO BECOMING EXTRAORDINARY

To begin developing our Best Self we need to gather information about how other people experience us when we are at our best. This type of feedback is rare and critical in moving toward a sense of equivalence in how we perceive ourselves and how others perceive us. For Hope, identifying a Best Self moment came easily. But what if you're not sure when you're acting in your Best Self?

Here is the process I invite you to try.

Identify at least six people who know you well, whom you respect, and who are invested in your success. Send them an e-mail. Let them know that you are conducting a personal development survey and that their observations and input are important to you right now. Ask them the following questions:

1. Tell me about a time(s) when you saw me at my best. Please write a brief narrative that describes how I showed up, how I approached problem solving, how I dealt with challenges, etc.

2. What words come to mind when you think about me in this situation(s)?

3. In what ways did I influence the people and environment around me?

4. What were the qualities, attributes and strengths that I brought to this time that you most appreciated in me?

5. In what new situations could I put these strengths into use?

After you receive the feedback, take the time to sit with it for a while. Identify some of the themes and insights that emerge from the information. Boil down these thoughts and impressions from outside sources into a few simple sentences that inform how you think, feel, and behave when other people experience you at your best.

_____

_____

_____

If you think about Hope's experience as a musician, she developed four keys or sense memories that, for her, triggered a state of positivity and confidence. Each of these represent a physical, mental, emotional, and energetic element. Try this for yourself.

Think of two or three moments or experiences in your life when you've felt in your Best Self. These will be times when you felt most alive, confident, energized, and effective.

_____

_____

_____

What was the physical posture or stance that represented you during these Best Self moments? This is your *Signature Stance*.

_____

_____

_____

How did you feel emotionally at these times? (Examples: Courageous? Playful?)

_____

_____

_____

Describe your energy at these times? (Examples: Calm? Exuberant?)

_____

_____

_____

What was your mindset at these times? (Examples: Adaptable? Generous?)

_____

_____

_____

Try to identify three or four memories that trigger a state of positivity and confidence. (Examples: Your bow at the end of your best performance. The breath you take before stepping onto the pitcher's mound.)

_____

_____

_____

Some people may find it easier than others to remember and recapture their Best Self. For others there may be an unidentified barrier that prevents them from feeling fully confident. It's OK if discovering your own keys doesn't come easily. It's really hard to do it alone. But with effort, it can be done. As you'll read next, it takes courage and openness to rediscover and reclaim one's personal power.

HEALING AN OLD WOUND

Setbacks are a part of every artist's journey. It is precisely our formative training and experience that provides us with a place to land, recoup, and reemerge. But what happens when we lose our confidence completely and do not have a road map back to our Best Self?

A colleague and close friend of mine, Christo, is a gifted executive coach in Philadelphia with a unique story. We met at a time when he was searching for something that he had lost, his self-confidence.

While carpooling one day, Christo shared that he sometimes lost his confidence in front of more senior colleagues in the consulting company where he works. Though he was quite capable in his area of expertise, for some reason he would periodically just lose his focus and crumble in front of his colleagues.

I asked him when this all started. He paused, and as he focused and reflected I saw his jaw tighten. Then he got a little choked up and shared his story with me.

Christo grew up in South Africa and was a gifted cricket bowler, a fast bowler to be precise. (This is equivalent to a fast ball pitcher in baseball.) By the time he was 10 years old, he'd drawn the attention of recruiters and was on the track to becoming a professional.

"One afternoon I was playing for fun with some kids at school. The match was close and a big kid from the other team stepped up to bat.

"I was tall for my age, but this kid was taller and larger than me," Christo explained. "It didn't matter, I was unfazed and bowled with confidence. I executed my pitches and successfully 'dismissed [struck out]' the other kid. I was elated."

That's when, in a fit of rage, the other kid sprinted to Christo and savagely pounded his fist into his face, so hard that Christo slumped to the ground, dazed.

By his facial expression, his body language, and the emotion in his voice, I could see Christo was fully reliving this moment in his life.

"I jumped to my feet," he continued, "disoriented and shamed. I wanted to punch him back, but I had nothing left inside of me. I just turned and ran away."

He'd repressed this story for a long time, but Christo realized that this was the exact moment he lost his "mojo." After the attack, he never summoned the same power or confidence as a fast bowler again.

As a young cricket player, Christo knew what he was doing. He was capable, competent, and confident. But when the other kid punched him, it challenged everything he thought he knew about himself. Unconsciously, when he would speak in front of more senior colleagues, that traumatic moment would return to him and he would shrink inside of himself.

When we arrived at our destination, Christo turned to me and, with deep gratitude, thanked me. He radiated relief and a sense of excitement and determination. He knew that he needed to come to terms with this moment in his life, forgive himself, and reclaim his power.

DON'T LEAVE THE BEST BEHIND

Deborah Ancona, Founder of the MIT Leadership Center at MIT, has a powerful question that she asks students: "What is the part of yourself that you left behind to become the person you are today?" How would you answer this question?

_____

_____

_____

Everyone has the potential to be extraordinary. Everyone can reclaim their gifts—even when they feel as though they've fallen into a slump or lost their spark. Becoming extraordinary requires looking inward and doing the work. It's a matter of drawing out and realizing the intrinsic value of that specific part of ourselves. It's not always easy, but it will always be worth the effort. When we truly understand what it means to be our Best Self, we open the door to endless possibilities. We also begin to see the best in others and strive to create a space for them to be their Best Self.

2

THE ART OF LANDING

Tension is who you think you should be.
Relaxation is who you truly are.
—PROVERB

When he was in his twenties, Pat was an overly polite and eager sales executive. He always wanted to please others while also behaving and
speaking like the ideal leader—to a fault because it actually interfered with his
client work. His boss would often chide him, saying, "Pat, don't be so uptight,
relax. It's OK. Just be the person you are when we go out for a drink together."

Though we only spoke briefly, Pat's experience resonated with me as a
common challenge for people working to develop their executive presence.
Have you had a similar experience, where you find it easy to communicate in
some situations but tense up when you feel the heat is on? Has a supervisor
urged you to "relax and just be yourself" during professional exchanges?

In this chapter we'll discuss the notion of "landing" as the foundation for
building executive poise, presence, and influence. *Landing is the experience of
being fully grounded and present in our bodies.* Leaders skilled at landing are
self-regulated and capable of staying calm and centered in new situations
without awkwardness or embarrassment. They are comfortable in their own
skin and show up without affectation or pretense. Landing means more than
just putting on a game face. It is a quality of graciousness and responsiveness
that puts others at ease while still able to make decisions under immense pressure and constant change.

SIGNALS OF PRESENCE

From the perspective of an actor or performing artist, the development of executive poise, presence, and influence begins with two things: how you show up and the message you send without saying a word. Whenever we interact with others, we give off signals. These signals are found in our voice, facial gestures, emotions, and body language.

In order to gain a better understanding of these signals, let's look at them from the viewer's perspective. Think about someone in your organization or community who exhibits executive poise and presence, then answer the following questions.

What words come to mind when you think about them?

_____

_____

_____

Describe their energy. Is it scattered, frenetic, calming, etc.?

_____

_____

_____

How do they show up physically and emotionally?

_____

_____

_____

Are they present and focused? Why or why not?

_____

_____

_____

Describe the quality of their eye contact.

_____

_____

_____

Do they seem comfortable in their own skin? Why or why not?

_____

_____

_____

Are they approachable? Why or why not?

_____

_____

_____

Identifiable Markers

Now that you have gathered some data of your own, let's see what we find. The leaders that you have identified likely exhibit some of the following:

- They are fully present and engaged.
- They have excellent posture, stand tall, and exude confidence.
- They are relaxed and comfortable in their own skin. They are composed.
- They have a steady, open, and personal gaze. They don't seem distracted or have any extraneous movements.
- They fill the room with their presence. It is palpable. They also seem approachable, not guarded.
- When they speak, their communication is congruent—in other words, their face, body, voice, and emotions all send the same message.

The leaders you analyzed likely possess an executive presence that says most of the following: *I want to be here. I believe in what I am saying. I care about you. I am willing to listen.* Were these leaders born with executive poise and presence? Most likely not. It comes with experience, awareness, and training, all of which you have access to as well.

Congruence

Developing executive poise, presence, and influence starts with the story that we tell ourselves. Do you remember my story in the Introduction about how my need to be liked fell away while I was performing? This discomfort is the gap between our real self and an unrealistic ideal self. As Manuela Herbele points out:

> If the way that I am (the real self) is aligned with the way that I want to be (the ideal self), then I will feel a sense of mental well-being or peace of mind. If the way that I am is not aligned with how I want to be, the incongruence, or lack of alignment, will result in mental distress or anxiety. The greater the level of incongruence

between the ideal self and real self, the greater the level of resulting distress.[1]

In other words, we feel viscerally uncomfortable when we make decisions and act out of alignment with our Best Self. Let's apply this concept to Pat's situation at the beginning of the chapter. He noticed that he was comfortable in informal settings. In such situations, Pat's communication style was confident and expressive, and the way his peers perceived him was in tune with the way he wanted to be seen.

However, when he stepped into his sales role at work, Pat acted in the way he thought he "should" show up, and it came off as awkward and uncomfortable. This inauthentic persona created tension and insecurity that was felt and experienced by others.

In the short term, Pat's awkward presence impacted how his clients experienced him. The long-term consequences could have been even more serious.

Trap of the Professional Persona

In the mid-2000s I was delivering a session for Ernst & Young, a large consulting firm. In one of the exercises I needed a leader to step in front of the group of 80 consultants and share an issue or problem with which he was struggling.

My volunteer was a tall man, impeccably dressed and clearly very uncomfortable. But he committed to the opportunity to be vulnerable in front of his organization. As he walked out, he slowly took off his suit coat and unbuttoned his collar. He took a deep breath, let it out, smiled, and then started to speak. He was honest and transparent as he described the situation with which he was wrestling. His sense of vulnerability had an immediate impact on the group and opened up a spirited conversation.

Being vulnerable in front of others is a tough practice. It's easy to talk about problems after you've solved or conquered them. But to reveal and open them up for discussion while you're struggling (with no guarantee that you'll eventually succeed) demands bravery.

After the session this leader came up to me and expressed his gratitude. He said, "Today I learned a powerful lesson on what leadership is truly about. For the past 20 years I have been working hard to build a professional persona as a leader. It was like a veneer, an impenetrable shield that I wore to work. I worked hard to be seen as a model of perfection, as someone with all of the answers." He continued, "It has always felt like a burden, and I have never felt comfortable with it. I now realize it was all pretense. I like who I am, and I'm definitely not perfect. Just ask my wife. If we are going to bring out the best in ourselves and others, and achieve the best outcomes, we need to be honest and transparent with each other and with our clients. This was a great first step. Thank you!"

Strive for Excellence, Not Perfection

The business person in the story above had convinced himself that there was a particular way an executive "should" look and behave. He might as well have hung a sign over his door that read: "Leave your personality at the door."

> **Leave your PERSONALITY at the door.**

For more than 20 years he carried around the burden of trying to be "perfect." This moment in my program finally allowed him to take down the sign and make a significant shift in how he had been showing up as a leader. He began the journey of shifting his focus from perfection to excellence, because when we strive for excellence we lead from our Best Self.

LET GO AND LAND

The executive from this story also succeeded in letting go of an unrealistic image of perfection that he had created for himself. By accepting the challenge to be vulnerable in front of his larger team, he stepped forward and created a *Trial by Fire* experience (you'll recall from Chapter 1 that this is an experience that builds your integrity). In confidence, he told me that it was one of the most difficult things he had ever done. He felt terrified and thought he might be laughed out of the room. But he faced his fear.

To the audience, he did not lose any of his status as a leader. When he took the risk to be vulnerable, his credibility and authenticity increased. Are you someone who also feels that you need to have all the answers? How difficult would it be for you to step into the fire like this leader did?

A MINDSET OF EXCELLENCE

The executive above left his personality at the door and repressed his real self. However, this doesn't mean that we should show up to work in our pajamas. There is a balance between putting on a facade and not bringing your A game.

I've worked with more than a few folks who seem to equate authenticity with a sense of relaxed disregard. This mentality often shows up in the way they dress, the language that they use, and how they regard the power structure within which they work. One does not have to put on a power suit and bark orders to be seen as a leader. But one does need to understand the norms of our domain while finding ways to be true to our values and be our Best Self.

If we think back to Hope's story from Chapter 1, we see that it was precisely her training, discipline of practice, and *Trials by Fire* that created the experience of being her Best Self. She possessed a mindset of excellence and was then able to successfully access and bring these best parts of herself to her role at work. Being your Best Self comes out of discipline, practice, and trial and error.

. . .

Let's take a moment to explore the mindset of excellence.

Describe a time when you showed up as the person you wanted to be.

_____

_____

_____

Describe how you felt at this time.

_____

_____

_____

Describe how others responded to you.

_____

_____

_____

Describe a time when you were unable to show up as the person you wanted to be.

_____

_____

_____

Describe how you felt at this time.

_____

_____

_____

Describe how others responded to you.

_____

_____

_____

COMMITMENT TO ACTION

Building awareness of the disconnect between being the person that others truly appreciate and being the person we think we "should" be is an important step in the process of becoming one's Best Self. However, finding a way to bridge this gap can be daunting and anxiety provoking.

Understanding the emotion of fear is crucial in landing fully inside of ourselves. In an *Inc.* magazine article titled "The Only Thing You Need to Do to Overcome Fear, According to Neuroscience," Mareo McCracken pointed out that fear and anxiety are rooted in uncertainty about the future—the fear of not being good enough or smart enough. It has been proven that the human brain cannot focus on more than one thing at a time. So, this means that moving past fear is a matter of choice and rests in our own hands. To displace our fear, we simply need to refocus our minds. "The only thing you need to do," notes McCracken, "is make a commitment. Why? Commitment means an action is taking place and your brain is focusing on something else besides the fear."[2] Turning our attention to our breath or engaging in an act of kindness and generosity are just two small examples of action that can help us outsmart our fears.

If you look back at the story about the executive from Ernst & Young who was afraid of being mocked, you will see that he was committed to stepping in front of the audience and facing his fear. Once he stepped into the fire and got into action, his fear was neutralized. His commitment guided him forward. Commitment to change is the first step in taking action. Our brains are focused on the activity and fear is displaced.

CONNECTING TO OUR BREATH

How does someone maintain composure under stress? Let's look at how Navy SEALs are trained. They have a process that focuses on developing skills and then putting these skills to test under high-stress conditions. Again, *Trials by Fire.* They start developing self-regulation skills by learning how to control their breathing patterns.

Connecting to our breath is the most fundamental principle for developing poise and presence. It is an essential way for us to land fully inside of ourselves. By paying attention to and regulating our breathing, we learn to discover deep relaxation. This in turn allows us to access the best parts of ourselves and enables us to be fully in the present moment.

This process begins by becoming aware of when we hold our breath or feel tension. The tension experienced from everyday stressors can build up without us noticing how it's affecting our body, which may include negative breathing patterns. And overtime carrying this tension and experiencing irregular breathing patterns can become the norm. In order to stop this from happening, we need to begin a process of releasing this tension.

Finding Your Belly Breath

Let me take you through a foundational breathing exercise: belly breathing. First, sit down tall in a chair with your feet flat on the floor and back against the chair. Let your hands and arms rest on your lap. Place your tongue on the roof of your mouth directly behind your top teeth. (This positioning of your tongue is a centering technique that stimulates the flow of energy and makes it harder to form words in your mind.)

Breathe in through your nose and out through your mouth.

Put your attention to your abdomen (belly) and breathe out all of the air in your lungs. As you breathe out, let your belly deflate as though you were squeezing all of the air out of a rubber ball.

Now, pause.

Then allow your breath to enter in through your belly and try to keep your shoulders from rising.

Pause at the top of your breath and begin to breathe out.

Repeat this at least 10 times.

When you are done, notice how you feel. Is your body relaxed? Is your mind more focused? Try it again.

If you have difficulty finding your "belly breath" and notice your shoulders rising up, try this. Lie down flat on your bed and lift your knees up, keeping your feet flat. (This might not work so great in your office unless you close the door.)

Place your hands on your belly or belt buckle and do the same sequence.

If you practice this once or twice a day for two weeks, you will discover a relaxation point.

. . .

This is a foundational breathing exercise, but it's also a master exercise. Do not underestimate the power that can come from developing this type of essential breathing practice. If you have not done this before, remember that you are a novice. It is very easy to try it once and dismiss it because it did not immediately work for you. Practice is the admission to mastery.

Breathe-Connect-Land

Sometimes it helps to have a short and memorable breathing sequence. The sequence that I created and use is *Breathe-Connect-Land*, and it builds upon the same belly-breathing technique that we just learned.

As you breathe in, say the word "Breathe" to yourself. When you get to the top of your breath say the word "Connect" to yourself, focus on feeling centered, and let go of any tension. Then begin to breathe out and say the word "Land" to yourself. Let all of the tension you hold flow out through your feet. Try this at least 10 times.

Building a Meditation Practice

I was first introduced to meditation while studying abroad in Nepal and India during my junior year in college. Over the years that followed, I have incorporated many other forms of breathing and meditation exercises into my life. The interesting thing is that the older I get, the more I rely on these daily practices. Below are some of the practices as well as the benefits from developing a daily breathing and meditation practice.

- **Create a morning ritual.** I get up and immediately drink two glasses of water. I then make myself a cup of tea and straightaway sit in my meditation chair for at least 20 minutes and up to 50 minutes.

- **Find what works for you.** Every person is wired differently. For those who have a high-frequency nervous system, like me, I recommend starting your meditations with deep breathing exercises. For those who need to develop empathy and connection, I recommend more heart-based exercises found in Tibetan loving-kindness. And for those who struggle with anxiety, core mindfulness exercises are very effective.

- **Wait for it.** I have discovered that there is a clear space that is waiting for you in your meditation if you are patient. With diligent practice you will be able to unlock your innate positivity, which is an energy that flows naturally within all of us. I find that it actually displaces any negative thoughts and feelings I may be experiencing.

. . .

I rely on my daily practice of breathing and meditations to manage stress, overcome insecurity, and open up strategic thinking. If practiced in the mornings, it is much easier to get centered and reestablish a positive mindset during your day.

If you like, you can visit my website for a short video in which I will lead you through a variety of breathing and meditation exercises that you can incorporate into your daily routines (www.leadingfromyourbestself.com /resources).

PRESENCE IS A CHOICE

Building self-awareness about the internal and external forces that are pulling at our attention is the most powerful way to get present with others.

Answer the following questions for yourself.

- What percent present are you right now? Give each of the following a number: physically, mentally, and emotionally.

- What is keeping you from being here 100 percent?
  - Are you thinking about something that happened in the past? Are you thinking about something that you have coming up?
  - Do you have a personal issue that needs to be resolved?
  - Are you waiting for a phone call?
  - Are you anxious to check your e-mail?

Countless things can keep us from being in the present moment. In order to avoid distraction we must learn to acknowledge the situation and the feelings it causes, and decide whether we need to deal with it right now or put it aside to be dealt with later. By consciously acknowledging what we are holding on to or what is pulling on us, the hold it has on us automatically diminishes.

Team Check-In

The following e-mail exchange happened between myself and the COO of a startup in Boston who attended one of my sessions. He liked the "What percent present are you right now?" exercise and decided to use it with his team. The effect was positive but brought up some additional questions.

Initial e-mail:

Rob,

Good afternoon, and I hope you've had a good week. Have a curveball for you, a coaching question based on your program from a few weeks ago . . .

One of the tools that I've implemented is asking each team member what % present they are at the start of our weekly team meeting.

It's had a great response, people love it. From a management perspective it's great as you get a unique view into how your employees operate.

This question came up today: if someone has a low %, say 40%, and they explain why (bad night of sleep, stressed about sales numbers, bad call with customer, etc.) should we address that at the meeting or take it offline? I suspect it depends on the topic (personal or work-related) but would love your thoughts on this.

Thanks,

CW

My response:

Hi CW,

Thank you for reaching out with your question. Let me say first that you have done a great job of applying the learning from the program. As we discussed, your role is to not only be present for others, but to enable them to be fully present as well.

By asking them the question about % present, you were able to focus their attention and got a glimpse into how each of them was thinking and feeling. However, you don't want to derail the purpose of the meeting.

Let's look at your situation.

- First, the best way to respond to a team member when they are less than optimally present might be with a question (be curious—inquire). It seems to me that you might be looking for one of two things:

  1. Do they have something looming over them that needs to be addressed at this very moment? (For instance, a client needs an answer within 30 minutes)

  2. Do they have a more global or general issue like dealing with anxiety, lack of sleep, bad call with a customer, or stress about the numbers?

- It might also be helpful to set up the purpose of the "What % present are you right now?" with them and empower them to be more self-aware. If they come to the meeting and are distracted because something needs their immediate attention, they need to let the team know what is going on and deal with it. This is fully acceptable. Just don't make it a habit.

- If it is something of a more general nature, ask them to bring the issue to your attention in advance, if possible.

- If it happens in the moment, first acknowledge and legitimize their discomfort. Then ask things like:

  ○ Would you be willing to share what is distracting you?

  ○ Is it something that you can put aside for the moment and focus on the task at hand?

  ○ Would you like to discuss this in a one-on-one setting?

- If the individual is showing signs of visible discomfort, you need to decide if it is critical enough to deal with in the moment. You may want to ask them if they would like to take the time to collect themselves in private. This question might jar them enough to get them to focus and join the meeting. Most importantly, always follow up with them if the issue sounds important.

- If other team members seem to be struggling with the same issue, it could be a good general learning session. Set aside a time to introduce the following:

- ○ Breathing techniques:
  - • To create a sense of positivity and counteract the effects of a bad meeting.
  - • To release the stress and tension from the day and get a good night's sleep.
- ○ Communication techniques:
  - • To ask for help when you are feeling the stress of making the numbers.

Let me know if these thoughts are helpful to you. Glad to discuss in more depth.

Enjoy the wintery weather.

Rob

The e-mail exchange with CW above demonstrates a commitment to learning by taking a skill practiced in a class and putting it into action right away. CW found immediate positive results from the activity, and also discovered that it takes experimentation and responsive leadership to bring about great results.

· · ·

Thinking back to the various skills presented in this chapter, how will you demonstrate a commitment to learning?

I encourage you to take a moment and reflect upon the following questions. Digging deep into your own patterns of presence (good and bad) and building awareness can help you change your less-than-effective habits.

In what situations could you be more present with others?

_____

_____

_____

What attitudes, behaviors, and actions can you put into practice to get fully present?

_____

_____

_____

Where could you put *Breathe-Connect-Land* into practice?

_____

_____

_____

What would be the payoff to implementing *Breathe-Connect-Land*?

_____

_____

_____

How can you create the conditions for others to be fully present?

_____

_____

_____

Listen with Your Eyes!

Giving another person your full and undivided attention is one of the greatest gifts you can give. It is also one of the most powerful aspects of presence. I would like to share a story from Dan Collier, senior manager of leadership and professional development at Fresenius Medical Care and president of the Boston chapter of the Association for Talent Development.

> During my daughter, Lauren's, early school years, I chose to work from home so that I could meet her at the bus and bring her home each day. We developed a habit of talking about her day during the walk from the bus, which continued till I settled her in the room next to my home office. Most days, I could afford to dedicate attention to her kindergarten stories and adventures. However, one day, I had a very important project consuming my attention. I barely acknowledged Lauren during the walk home. As I got her settled in the room next to mine, my attention was elsewhere.
>
> After a few disingenuous "Uh uhs," "that's nices," and "good for yous," I noticed her monologue of the day's activities had stopped. Before I could look over to ensure she hadn't gotten into something, I felt her hands hold my cheeks and turn my head toward her while saying, "No Daddy, listen with your eyes." As someone who teaches communication skills for a living, being told by a five-year-old to "listen with my eyes," was an epiphany.

Can you think of a time when someone gave you their undivided attention? They listened with their eyes? How did this make you feel? How would you describe the quality of their presence? Similarly, can you think of a time when someone was "uh-huh-ing" you? What effect did that have on you?

CULTIVATING POISE AND COMPOSURE

Between stimulus and response there is a space. In that space is our power to choose our response. In our response lies our growth and our freedom.
—VICTOR FRANKL

It's one thing to maintain composure when times are easy and everyone is amicable. But what about when everyone at the conference table is sniping at each other and reasonable discussion's gone out the window? Or when a co-worker throws you a curveball? In such high-pressure and contentious situations it can be very easy to become reactive—acting in response to a situation rather than creating or controlling it. When we're in reactive mode, we're more likely to get swept up in the emotional heat of the moment and fly off the handle. That rarely helps anyone on a personal or professional level.

This is where breathing techniques can be exceptionally helpful. That might sound strange, but practicing your breathing can help you relax, focus, and stay grounded even when the heat is on. Commitment to a breathing practice can't be understated. You don't need to move away to the mountains and immerse yourself in a breathing boot camp. Even just practicing 10 minutes a day (every day, mind you) can make a huge difference.

Over time, you'll notice something amazing happen. You'll get used to making the most fundamental of choices: to breathe. That will have a ripple effect, and you'll begin to notice all the other small but significant moments in your life when you have a choice. Your everyday awareness will widen. You'll be able to stay composed and above the fray, rather than being sucked in and getting defensive. You'll remain composed during tense moments and capable of observing the behaviors of your coworkers. By not getting emotionally invested in a squabble or tense moment, you'll be free to take control of the moment and advance the conversation to more productive outcomes.

Breathing is a great start but improving your situational awareness can also be aided by identifying your values and triggers. For instance, your values might include respecting and building upon the ideas of others, to invite and hear all voices, and to be open to an outcome greater than one's personal point of view.

Identifying what's important to you in a work environment helps make you more aware when one of your values feels violated (such as in a combative team discussion where no one listens to each other) and you're likely to snap or shut down.

Getting a handle on your values, triggers, and reactions is important because they're your source for building awareness. They're your own clues to staying grounded. Everything you need is inside of you. Working through the questions that follow will help you increase your self-awareness and your skill-building capabilities.

What are your top three workplace values?

1. _____

2. _____

3. _____

What are the things that trigger you?

_____

_____

_____

How do you tend to react when you get triggered?

_____

_____

_____

THE BENEFITS ARE UNDENIABLE

By choosing to take up and practice the techniques laid out in this chapter, we open ourselves to a wealth of benefits. We are able to maintain poise, access our critical thinking skills more quickly, and remain objective and regulated during the most stressful interactions and decisions we make.

Now, we are better able to:

- **Read our audience**—interpret the facial expressions and mannerisms of others.

- **Connect the dots**—analyze and infer the meanings behind the words and read between the lines.

- **Suspend judgment**—pause and gather more data before jumping to biased conclusions, decisions, and actions.
- **Change our point of view**—take on multiple perspectives and see the implications and consequences of our actions more clearly.

All of these skills form the basis for building critical thinking skills and leadership agility. The Agile Leader is one that is poised and responsive to an ever-changing business environment and able to make clear and rational decisions in a timely manner.

3

THE ART OF EXPANDING

Once you have found your own voice,
the choice to expand your influence, to increase your contribution,
is the choice to inspire others to find their voice.
—STEPHEN COVEY

The art of expanding is about how we show up in relationship with others. Our practice of expanding can grow if we look at it in layers of experience. Consider the following:

- How others experience us
- How others experience themselves when they are with us
- The story others tell about us when we are gone

As we start to develop and expand our presence we begin to notice the impact that it has on others. When we put our attention to this impact we learn to expand into the experience of others. Our growth as a leader and effective communicator arises out of this awareness.

HOW OTHERS EXPERIENCE US

People can experience us in a number of ways. So, let's break this down.

- **Energetically.** We all have a signature energy that others experience when they are with us. This is the first thing that others experience of us and that has an immediate impact on them. We might project a sense of calm that instills confidence in others or a frenetic energy that puts everyone on edge. With feedback and practice we can become aware of the energy we project when we are at our best and our worst. Questions to consider:

- Are you aware of the energy that you project in different situations?

- How could you better manage your energy?

- **Physically.** Our physical presence is also something that creates an impact on others. Some of us have an imposing physical presence that stifles others. Some are less commanding in our physical presence yet radiate confidence. With discipline, training, and awareness we can learn to develop a stature that is strong, flexible, and approachable—our *Signature Stance*. Questions to consider:

  - Are you aware of your facial gestures and body language?

  - When are you at your most physically expressive?

- **Emotionally.** Some of us reveal our full range of emotions in the moment for everyone to see and experience, while others wear a permanent poker face. Neither is optimal. Gaining awareness and control of our emotions in the workplace is critical, especially in high-pressure situations and as we ascend into higher organizational ranks. This awareness is the first step in developing emotional intelligence. Questions to consider:

  - Are you aware of the range of emotions that you have during your day?

  - What is the impact that your emotions have on others?

- **Vocally.** The quality and tone of our voice also communicates layers of meaning. Great communication comes from understanding how the voice, body, energy, and emotions work together to send messages that are congruent and resonate with authenticity and meaning. Questions to consider:

  - Do you speak in a monotone?

  - How could you use a range of inflection when you speak to clarify a key point?

- **Relationally.** Others also experience us in a relational manner. They experience us as being present, approachable, and trustworthy, or as distant and aloof. Questions to consider:
    - Are you aware of the relational impact you have on others?
    - How does it enable or obstruct you from a successful interaction?
    - How does it help or prevent you from building trust?

- **Intellectually.** Depending upon our biases or conditions under which we work, we can be protective or generous with our ideas. Some of us might project a sense of intellectual superiority, while others project inclusivity and humility. Questions to consider:
    - Do you wear a chip on your shoulder? Where does this come from?
    - How could you appreciate the value that someone else brings to the table?

Understanding how others experience you is important, because impressions that you leave with others affect their response to your leadership and your ideas. In order to consider the impressions that others have of us, let's take a moment to answer the questions below.

How do others experience you? Think back to the feedback that you received from the Best Self activity in Chapter 1. Look at the list below and pick your top three.

Adaptable	Calm	Diligent	Flexible	Impatient	Lethargic	Poised
Affectionate	Caustic	Distant	Focused	Insecure	Manic	Positive
Approachable	Confident	Distracted	Frantic	Intense	Open	Rational
Authentic	Connecting	Encouraging	Generous	Intuitive	Optimistic	Reliable
Boorish	Controlling	Energizing	Gracious	Jaded	Overbearing	Sincere
Brilliant	Demanding	Engaged	Humble	Kind	Passionate	Trusting

What insight does this give you about your presence?

_____

_____

_____

HOW OTHERS EXPERIENCE THEMSELVES WHEN THEY ARE WITH US

Our ability to expand into our own experience as well as the experience of others is critical to our development of empathy and our growth as a leader.

Feeling Small

Have you ever felt small in someone else's presence? I would imagine the answer is yes. It could be that moment at a gathering when you walk up to a senior leader you have always wanted to meet, and the person looks right through you like you don't even exist. Or, when you finally summon up the courage to speak at the team meeting, only to have your point reiterated by your boss with no reference to or acknowledgment of your previous contribution.

How did this make you feel? Undervalued, insignificant, or maybe even worthless? When we feel small it is very difficult to access our Best Self.

Let's examine a quote from a Harvard Business School Professor Joshua Margolis:

> *Leadership is about how someone else experiences*
> *themselves in your presence.*

Reflect on this for a moment. What does it mean to you?
Write down your thoughts.

_____

_____

_____

Below are some of the thoughts and impressions I have received from leaders over the years about what this quote means to them:

- Leadership is about others and the impact that we have on them.
- As leaders we need to be curious about what others are experiencing.
- As a leader, do I cast a shadow or turn on a light for others?

We need to notice when something is not right but nothing is being said. We do this by tuning into the other person's energy, body language, and facial expressions, and then having the courage to invite people to share their thoughts.

42

Let's examine a simple interaction at work to see how differently a situation can play out based on a leader's engagement.

You knock on the door of your boss's office and ask her if she has a moment. "Sure, come on in," she says, working away at her computer. When you enter she turns slightly and asks how she can help you, but never takes her eyes off what she is doing. You have something important to share with her, but you can see that this might not be the best time.

Unfortunately, your boss does not fully turn her attention to you. What do you do in this situation? Do you speak up and ask for her attention, or do you shrink back out of the door and let it go?

I am sure that you have been on both sides of this interaction at one time or another. On the one hand, it is critical for managers to learn to be present and open with others and be able to shift their attention from doing to relating, from the tactical to the relational. Realizing the significance of these moments is an important awareness for leaders to build. On the other hand, it is equally important to those asking for attention to develop a solid foundation of self-worth and learn to choose their moments well.

Limiting Negative Self-Talk

Feeling small is something that many of us carry inside of ourselves. And in some instances, the other person only serves as a trigger for our own self-limiting thoughts. In the example of the distracted manager, this already deep-seeded belief of *I'm not important, and my time is not important* is just confirmed.

These self-limiting thoughts are often a direct result of our upbringing, experiences, or academic training. It is drilled into us that if we want to get to the top we need be close to perfect and the smartest person in the room. If not caught early in one's career, these self-limiting *thoughts* can turn into self-limiting *beliefs*. This mindset can hold us back or warp us into adopting negative coping behaviors that impact our effectiveness in the workplace.

Feeling Large

Have you ever felt large in someone else's presence? I would also expect the answer is yes. Can you describe the feeling? Do you feel engaged, respected, and valued for your contributions? What did the person say or do that made you feel this way?

When we feel large, we experience ourselves as expanded, confident, and open and we are better able to access our Best Self.

One day I had to make an introduction to a class in the Harvard Business School Executive Education program. I stepped up in the back of the auditorium and caught the attention of the professor. He was the faculty chair of the program, a finance guy, and someone who was funny and a bit nerdy. He saw me in the back of the room and waved.

The class was engaged in an activity, and it was difficult for him to focus their attention, so he reached back, grabbed a plastic bottle of sparkling water on his desk, and banged it on the table like a gavel. The bottle exploded all over him. He and everyone in the class immediately burst out laughing. The moment of absurdity relaxed and focused everyone. At this point everyone calmed down, and he proceeded to wave me down with a smile and introduce me. I stepped into his space feeling large and confident when making my introduction.

The professor was fully comfortable with himself, and this sense of self-acceptance garnered a deep respect from his students. He took his work seriously, but himself lightly. He had a presence that was both confident and approachable. It also allowed him to create a space for others to feel large, comfortable, and confident in themselves as well.

This sense of feeling large is directly connected to our sense of confidence. Many people who struggle with confidence often compare themselves to others. True confidence is honestly assessing your own value, experience, intelligence, and capabilities, while also valuing and respecting the capabilities and contributions of others.

I invite you now to reflect on your own experiences with confidence.

In what situations have you felt filled with confidence?

_____

_____

_____

_____

What were the contributing factors that influenced this feeling?

_____

_____

_____

_____

In what situations have you felt your confidence drain out of you?

_____

_____

_____

_____

What were the contributing factors that influenced this feeling?

_____

_____

_____

_____

THE STORY OTHERS TELL ABOUT US WHEN WE ARE GONE

In a recent leadership development program for a large European bank, I was responsible for coaching a group of four leaders. Prior to the program, I arranged an introductory phone call with each person. My first three conversations were open, engaged, and productive.

My fourth call was quite the opposite. It was with a Belgian leader, Franco. In our conversation, I experienced him as being closed, curt, and impatient. At the opening reception of the program, I was standing in a small circle with my group when Franco joined us. He was stiff and wearing his game face as he introduced himself. He seemed withheld, formal, and aloof. The others tried to engage him in conversation without any luck. They responded to his reserve by closing him off.

At the end of the three-day leadership program something remarkable happened. I sat in a circle with my group of four leaders for a final debriefing. I asked each of them to share both their initial and final impressions of each team member.

One of the leaders turned to Franco and said, "When we first met on our initial team call, you seemed a bit cold and arrogant. Then, when we met at the opening reception, you gave us the same impression. I felt disappointed, and because of this, formed an immediate negative impression of you and took everything you said for the first hour and threw it away. I disregarded it."

The leader continued, "However, after three full days of working together, I found you to be the most generous person on the team. You were fully engaged in the simulation, you helped us without asking, and you were the most open to feedback and personal growth."

So, what happened here?

It just so happens that Franco was uncomfortable with initial introductions and small talk. He is an introvert who allowed his discomfort to affect how he showed up in these situations. He was unaware of how much those initial moments impacted the opinions and stories that others formed about him. It wasn't until he actually started to work with his colleagues in real time that he started to relax and open up. Unfortunately, while this program showed Franco's true nature, many of us do not get a second chance to make a first impression.

.   .   .

As a way to expand into our learning edges, consider what aspects of your presence you could begin to develop to increase your positive impact. Write down a specific situation, how you currently show up, how you would like to show up, and what action you need to take to get there for each aspect of your presence.

Your Energy

- Situation: _____
- Current State: _____
- Desired State: _____
- Action to Take: _____

Your Physicality

- Situation: _____
- Current State: _____
- Desired State: _____
- Action to Take: _____

Your Emotions

- Situation: _____
- Current State: _____
- Desired State: _____
- Action to Take: _____

Your Voice

- Situation: _____
- Current State: _____
- Desired State: _____
- Action to Take: _____

Your Intellectual Mindset

- Situation: _____
- Current State: _____
- Desired State: _____
- Action to Take: _____

What would keep you from being able to expand your presence in the ways that you have described above?

_____

_____

_____

After completing these exercises you may find that you have some work to do. Perhaps you have more "feeling small" moments than you'd like over the course of a day. Don't let this overwhelm you. Expanding is truly an art—one that requires self-awareness and continual practice. And remember: expanding is a choice, one that will get easier the more you practice.

FINDING YOUR VOICE

Finding your voice is something that every person struggles with. Unfortunately, many work environments create unrealistically high expectations for their employees that make it difficult for them to get their voices heard. Over time, these conditions create a cycle of perfectionism and self-doubt. So how can we overcome these conditions and challenge both ourselves and the status quo and get our voices heard? Let's find out.

Put an X on the Calendar

Sometimes we need to trick ourselves in order to allow our true voices (and Best Selves) to emerge. One example of this "benign deception" technique derives from a coaching client at MIT. Before we started working together, Ashley's company transferred her from its office in Thailand to another in Shanghai, China. The staff at her new job were older and much more experienced than she was. The culture in this new organization was such that the boss did all the talking while the team members were expected to shut up. This was in stark contrast to the culture within which she was raised in Thailand where women and team members were encouraged to speak up. In this new meeting environment Ashley discovered a boss who tended to not acknowledge that she or her teammates were even in the room.

Ashley's mission was to take the reins of a small sales and marketing group of five people all co-located in one office in Shanghai. This group had all been working together for almost 15 years, and several of them had not talked to each other for a majority of that time. This baffled her. What could have happened to have caused these people who worked together day in and day out to be so fractured? She decided to have one-to-one conversations with each person and uncovered the backstory.

What she found was a history of bad management that resulted in favoritism, a lack of goals and expectations, and a cycle of blame and judgment. To correct this dysfunctional atmosphere, she began working with the group to identify all underlying issues and to create a joint revenue project between sales and marketing, as well as set expectations for both behavior and results.

Under this new plan the team began to work well together, and the project started to produce results. Ashley had done an excellent job as a leader, but after two and a half years she was getting exhausted. Her efforts had gone unacknowledged, and she still felt isolated and invisible with upper management.

Because her efforts were not being recognized, Ashley naturally decided she wanted to leave the company. However, because she did not want to forfeit her bonus, she took out her calendar and put an X on the exact date that would guarantee her compensation. With this date in mind, she made a promise to herself that she would not hold back her thoughts and opinions in front of her boss any longer. She would say exactly what was on her mind. She was going to leave a trail of fire behind her as she left.

Then something amazing happened. As Ashley began telling the truth and sharing her unvarnished point of view, others started to listen and pay attention. They too felt strengthened by her boldness.

After only a couple of months of this, senior management recognized the positive impact Ashley was having on her peers and team members and finally acknowledged her for her efforts. Because of the momentum she created, she barely noticed the X that she had put on her calendar and ended up remaining with the company for several more years.

What's most striking about this story is that Ashley discovered her voice when she made the decision to leave her job—when she felt that she had nothing to lose. By "deceiving" herself, she was free from any internal or external constraints and was finally able to speak out. And then when something remarkable happened, i.e., people *responded*, her bold, nothing-left-to-lose efforts blossomed into a true Best Self experience.

Of course, for many of us it's neither practical nor realistic to say whatever is on our minds without considering the consequences. But small actions that push against the status quo or add value to a conversation can make a big impact when it comes to finding our voice.

So, what "X" can you put on your calendar that will unleash your full and authentic voice? Some ideas to consider:

- **Have a point of view.** Adding value to a conversation can come in many forms. Being known for having a particular point of view can make you a valuable resource. Helping the team to consider an alternate opinion via a thoughtful question can often make the difference and eliminate costly mistakes.

- **Build upon someone else's idea.** Have you ever been ready to share an idea at a meeting only to have a colleague speak up before you with a similar thought? Rather than shrinking back, lean forward, acknowledge this person, and build upon the idea. Adding momentum to an idea is a powerful form of leadership.

- **Call for a pause in the action.** Taking a moment to share an observation about a comment that was glossed over or a conversation that has gone off track can help to bring awareness and keep a team on point.

Jot some ideas about how you might unleash your voice here:

_____

_____

_____

_____

THE JOURNEY HAS JUST BEGUN

Discovering your voice and expanding into the experience of others represent only the first steps in a much longer process of self-discovery and leadership development. But with a clear point of view and a solid foundation of values, principles, and unique leadership capabilities, you'll finally be ready for the next step: putting your voice to use while developing and refining your vision of yourself as a genuine and effective leader.

THE ART OF EXPANDING
INTO CONFLICT

Don't kid yourself, a conflict is never about the surface issue.
It's about one's unsaid, untreated, and unhealed wounds.
—ANONYMOUS

I n the last chapter we looked at the concept of expanding as a way to over-come feeling small, find our voice, and access our Best Self. We considered the notion of expanding into experience and developing an awareness of the way others experience us and themselves when they are with us. We learned how to expand beyond our comfort zone of communication and create environments that allow others to thrive.

In a perfect world, we could easily master the art of expansion consistently across many situations. But as anyone who operates in the working world knows, your Best Self and your ability to expand are constantly challenged.

You might have a coworker who seems to live to undermine you or a superior who only sees what you are doing wrong. You might also work in a culture that promotes competition to such a degree that it pits peer against peer. Whatever the case, most conflict has to do with difference. These differences can be opinions, backgrounds, gender, leadership styles, expectations, motivations, or personalities.

The art of expanding into conflict means learning to expand into difference even when your Best Self feels under threat. The challenge is how to stay large during moments of conflict.

The more we learn how to not only navigate through conflict, but actually expand into it, the more we realize the tremendous payoff in terms of honing reputation, building trust, reducing risk, and improving business results.

ROOTING OUT DYSFUNCTION STARTS WITH YOURSELF

Have you ever left a meeting where the group has agreed on a direction or commitment, and someone whispers, "That was a waste of time. It will never happen." I'm sure we all have—we may even have been the whisperer. Either way, these comments are undermining, destructive, and dysfunctional. When we experience them, we must expand into our Best Self and root out the damaging behaviors. We must also not be complicit when hearing them from others. We must confront the behavior, or simply ask a powerful question that opens up a truthful conversation.

Another helpful tactic would be to look into the reasons why you or members of your team do not feel comfortable enough to challenge or weigh in on the decisions during the open discussion. One of my favorite quotes is, "Leadership falls upon the most self-aware person in the room." Expanding into conflict is the art of acting upon that awareness in a positive and productive manner.

BUILDING RESILIENCE

Shame corrodes the very part of us that
believes we are capable of change.
—BRENÉ BROWN

What happens when it seems that the odds are stacked against you and you are unable to be your Best Self? How do you recover when things just don't go according to plan and you are the one left in the spotlight? How do you deal with not only embarrassment but feelings of shame?

You begin building your resilience.

Resilience is the art of recovery from traumatic incidents. As Brené Brown says, "It starts when we choose to walk inside of our own story and own it." Building resilience starts with a self-examination process. This step is crucial because you must understand what part you played in the drama and what was beyond your control. Next, you must reconnect with what is most important to you and your intrinsic value. You must remind yourself of the authentic contributions that you have made. Finally, you need to make the choice to expand and share your story. Again, as Brown explains, "If we can share our story with someone who responds with empathy and understanding, shame can't survive."[1] Sharing allows you to reenter your workplace, and your role within it, with confidence.

EPIC FAILURE—EPIC RECOVERY

It was early 2002 and I had been in my role as an account manager for a small training firm in Boston for a couple of years. We had just completed a project with a partnering consulting firm as a key resource on a large leadership development program. I was the lead on the project and had built up a solid reputation of dependability, agility, and performance under pressure. We were soon contacted by another member of the consulting firm to be a part of a pitch to a new and large client. Our CEO, my direct boss, immediately called a meeting and said I was to be a part of the pitch, but as a second to one of the principals of my organization. This was fine by me. However, we soon discovered that none of the principals were available to attend the meeting.

I immediately voiced a concern that I did not feel ready to go it alone. My comment was dismissed and the discussion continued. I voiced the concern a second time. Again, the discussion continued and a lukewarm solution was agreed on. When I voiced my concern a third time, I stood tall and accepted the role as primary agent from our organization.

The next day I arrived at the client location by myself. Upon entering the building, I met the consultant leading the pitch. We talked for a few minutes about the format of the pitch and I reiterated my concern, asking him to back me up in case things went south. He didn't seem to hear me, though I voiced my concern two more times with no acknowledgment.

The meeting was split into three parts. The first two went well, with both myself and the remote principal owning the pitch and delivering the goods. But once she hung up, the entire scenario could not have gone worse. The client asked me to bring our methodology to life. Being early in my tenure, I went into facilitation mode rather than remaining a strategic positioner. As much as I tried, I could not bring the conversation back on track. It was a slow crash and burn. I watched in horror as the consultant I'd asked to help me physically recoiled at the table and distanced himself from me. Upon leaving the meeting, one of the client's senior executives gave me words of encouragement, saying that we all have bad days.

I went home feeling decimated and continuously reminded myself of all of the reasons the meeting had failed. I started to have all kinds of thoughts, "Will I be fired?" "Will they take away my best accounts?" "How can I show my face in the office again?"

Instead of continuing down the dark tunnel, however, I reminded myself of my intrinsic value. I knew I had done everything in my power to create the conditions for success. I could have said no and not gone. But that is just not my style, nor would it have been a real option. I was determined not to let this break me.

In order to regain my footing, I went deeper and reconnected with my sense of purpose, which was to help others to develop their own self-confidence. While thinking about all of the great work I had been a part of over the last couple of years, I realized that I was living my purpose, and one way or another, I would continue to do it.

When I returned to the office the next day I had an opportunity to speak with the principal of our firm who was on the call. She was empathetic and kind and reassured me that things would be OK. She told me I did not have anything to worry about. The CEO kept his distance from me and sorted out the issues between the consultant and the potential client, and we eventually won the work, just not with me as the lead.

I did not let this deter me. It wasn't easy, but over the next two months, I stayed focused in my role and won the largest piece of work in the history of the company. The lessons I learned from the first unsuccessful meeting taught me so much and as a result helped me achieve this true moment of pride and accomplishment.

I received a valuable lesson during this time about perspective, resilience, and growth. I came out stronger.

After 12 years, I left this company, and in my exit interview with the CEO, he made a remark that stung. He said, "I never thought you were going to recover from that one." Lucky for me, I possessed the tools to bounce back on my own, but it would have made a huge difference if he had reached out during that stressful time.

Resilience is a learned art. Expanding is a learned art. Unbeknownst to the CEO, I had relied on my practice of both to succeed.

IT'S GOLD JERRY, IT'S GOLD!

"What do dashing Canadian prime minister Justin Trudeau and comedian Jerry Seinfeld have in common?" Zuri Davis asks this in her article, "Justin

Trudeau Shot Down a Heckler in a Town Hall, and Jerry Seinfeld Actually Responded." The answer: "Well, for one thing, they both have the same method for responding to hecklers."

When hecklers attempted to disrupt a town hall hosted by Trudeau, he didn't dismiss them, ignore them, or try to fight fire with fire. Rather, "Trudeau artfully engaged his hecklers, at one point asking the audience to give applause to the heckler for sharing their thoughts."[2]

Many writers linked Trudeau's empathetic approach to Jerry Seinfeld's, quoting from Seinfeld's Reddit AMA:

> Very early on in my career, I hit upon this idea of being the Heckle Therapist. So that when people would say something nasty, I would immediately become very sympathetic to them, and try to help them with their problem, and try to work out what was upsetting them, and try to be very understanding with their anger. It opened up a whole new, fun avenue for me as a comedian, and no one had ever seen that before. I would say things like, "you seem so upset, and I know that's not what you wanted to have happen tonight. Let's talk about your problem," to ease the outburst.[3]

Seinfeld's approach is about expanding into conflict. Both Seinfeld and Trudeau expand into conflict rather than closing themselves off. When fear, regret, loss, or some other kind of negative emotion has a tight hold on us, we can easily be triggered and project these unresolved feelings onto others. In most cases, resolution of conflict begins with building an awareness of and releasing our own negative emotions.

This is especially relevant for leaders.

Once leaders gain a deeper level of self-awareness and learn how to release negative emotions, they naturally become more empathetic and capable of expanding into the experience of another person. In turn, this gives them a much better path to dealing with conflict.

I have coached many people who, in the course of dealing with blame and conflict, have made assumptions and decisions based on partial information. If you do not know what is causing the disruption, be careful, be curious, lean in, and inquire. Develop your understanding of these types of situations and your ability to respond rather than react. Just as Jerry Seinfeld experienced early in his career, don't shy away from them, step into them. This approach will almost always defuse and deescalate contentious situations. It will demonstrate empathy and help to create a bridge of understanding and trust.

Let's say that you work in a technology-based organization and have deep expertise in helping large organizations through system-wide digital transformations. You and your team of highly trained engineers spend many months at the client's site. You work shoulder to shoulder with your client counterparts. Often, you discover deeper issues than what was initially scoped out in the project plan. What do you do? Do you just keep your head down, or do you courageously raise the issue with your key client? When clients realize that you are "all in" and always have their best interests in mind, you can truly earn their trust.

But what happens when that trust gets eroded? What happens when you find yourself and your team stuck in a cycle of blame and judgment? This is something that many organizations run up against from time to time while working on very complex engagements.

Let me share with you a case study of a recent client who was working on a digital transformation project with a large energy company. This story is told through the eyes of my client, Arshad.

From a Potential Lawsuit to a $6 Million Check

It is August 2016. For the past 18 months we had been leading a large-scale digital transformation project for an energy distribution company. During the prior six months issues had surfaced including missed milestones originating from both our side and the client side. With each delay the two teams sat down and renegotiated new milestones and began again. Our new launch date was now September, one month away.

We notified the client team of the change and received a new notice: "No way we can launch in September!"

We took a collective deep breath and proposed a November date. We felt confident that this would give both sides enough time to work through any issues and still hit this new target launch date.

We received yet another notice. This time they demanded that we take November off the table! Because they were facing their year-end close, it would be too much for them to handle both at the same time. Their proposed launch date was in March.

We were officially at a stalemate. There was no way we could wait until March! That was more than six months away, and it would put us way over budget. Plus, our credibility was on the line.

Our whole team was fuming, and I thought that if we did not resolve our differences quickly, we could be looking at a substantial lawsuit that would create chaos for both of us. I was feeling anxious beyond measure. The stakes were very high, and we needed to resolve this, and fast.

Meeting the Challenge

At this exact time I was enrolled in a class being delivered by Protagonist Consulting Group. On the first day of the program we were led through several experiential exercises designed to help us increase our influence with key stakeholders. These included how to be fully present and listen more deeply to the needs and concerns of others. One of my favorites was the use of a simple yet powerful self-regulation practice for getting into the present moment: *Breathe-Connect-Land*. It was as simple as it sounded. Take a deep breath in, connect with what is most important, then breathe out and land the intention inside of yourself. I would soon learn how important these tools would be in a subsequent call with my client.

That afternoon we worked on a model for open communication and dealing with conflict. It has four steps, *Observe-Think-Feel-Want* (O-T-F-W). The essence of the model is that people fall into the trap of blame and judgment when they are unable to disentangle their own experiences of conflict. People need to clearly reflect on the observable facts first, then on what they were thinking, then on the feelings that resulted from those thoughts, and finally on what they wanted or needed in that moment.

I willingly volunteered some issues I was having with my client for the class to examine. I started by giving some context. I outlined the recent interactions between the two working groups and mentioned the phone call I had scheduled first thing the following morning.

As we proceeded to move through the model, I started to project blame onto our client counterparts through the guise of feelings. I said that I felt deceived by what the client had been saying and then doing, and I was immediately reminded to stick to what I was actually feeling and not assign blame on the other party. I then experienced something remarkable: two opposing emotions about the unresolved situation. On one side, I was excited to see the light at the end of the tunnel on this project. On the other, I was concerned and discouraged that the two teams were at odds with each other with no obvious way forward.

I was then asked to repeat the process taking the point of view of our client. This proved to be an eye-opening process.

By taking the time to consider what my client had observed, thought, felt, and wanted, I was able to get out of my own myopic position on the situation. I was able to build true empathy for her situation.

It was by taking both points of view that I realized the root of the problem. We were operating from a fixed pricing structure. We were frustrated and blaming the client team for trying to squeeze out the most fixes and features from us and keeping us from our anticipated launch dates. We just wanted to get the framework up and running. In turn, the client team was blaming us for cutting corners and not bringing the most value to them.

Because of this disconnect, the teams were not aligned, mistrust was mounting, and we were losing our footing quickly.

I realized that the path forward hinged on communicating this paradox to my client. I left the session feeling confident in my approach for the call the next morning.

The Way Forward

That evening I began writing my thoughts out on paper. I was now better able to put myself in the shoes of my counterpart. I realized that, due to the fixed pricing structure we were operating under, my client had lost authority with her team. There was no incentive for her team to distinguish between the "nice to have" and "have to have" fixes and features. They no longer responded to her appeals and felt no sense of urgency to move forward. In addition, the steering committee was losing confidence in her ability to lead this project. In order to regain standing in the eyes of the committee, as well as regain influence with her team, she needed the right incentives in place, and the fixed pricing didn't provide that.

On our call, my goal was to frame a plan that would return authority to her. But before doing so, I knew I needed to build a relational bridge between us. I needed to be fully present on the phone with her and project a calm presence. Once on the call, the O-T-F-W model gave me a clear way to communicate our position to her without falling into the cycle of blame. I listened deeply in our conversation to see if she was experiencing the same paradox as me. She was able to see that the path to the finish line lay in changing the structure under which her team was operating. By the end of our call, we were able to get on the same page with the incentives and sense of urgency. The next step was for us to sit down with all of the key people and begin moving forward together. As it turned out, from her perspective, getting to the finish line was worth the outstanding $6 million that was owed to us. She initiated the payment immediately.

Sweet Victory

I arrived at the session on day two of the class at Protagonist Consulting Group and found the group already digging into a new exercise. Everyone turned and looked at me anxious to hear what had happened on my call. I was grinning from ear to ear. The key point I relayed to the group was that the model gave me a clear pathway to express my thoughts. I was able to acknowledge the miscommunication that had taken place over the last several months and expressed the impact that it was having on both of our teams. I was able to say this without blame. I was also able to say to my client the following: "All that we want is to move toward a successful launch, on time and on budget. I imagine that this is what you want as well?" She agreed. I then said, "I also imagine that you would like to be treated fairly in the process." She perked up in agreement. I then said, "This is also what we are looking for." For the first time in many months we were on the same side of the table agreeing on a positive way forward.

In essence, we were able to get beyond the cycle of blame and align on three key areas: the shared outcome, aligning on our values, and to be treated fairly. The final result was a win-win.

REFLECTIONS:
MOMENTS THAT MATTER

A couple of months after working with Arshad in my program, I was able to speak with him about how things had progressed with his client. He happily reported that he and his client continued to work collaboratively and launched the platform. It was the most successful launch ever. He also noted that several moments of truth had occurred that made a significant difference. One in particular was during an in-person meeting with the client when she took a moment to apologize to him for the way her team had been acting.

He expressed how much her words meant and, in turn, acknowledged his team's contribution to the problem. This was a powerful moment of connection between the two of them. She also told him that once the new commercial structure was in place, she had let her group know that the negative behavior had to stop, and that the steering committee was very impressed by her ability to move the project to a successful completion. He said that her whole presence and demeanor had changed. She stood taller, her voice was stronger, and she was much more relaxed inside of herself. It was not only a digital but a personal transformation as well.

Critical Communication Skills

The best businesses that lead full-scale transformation projects realize that the true nature of their work goes beyond their technical competence. Success comes from their ability to build and sustain quality relationships and resolve a multitude of interpersonal issues and conflicts with their clients that invariably crop up. These issues tend to take the form of differences in expectations, lack of communication, and a cycle of blame between parties. The deep-seated mistrust between the two teams in this case study was rooted in the misalignment of the pricing structure. It created different incentives for each team. It was not until authority was restored to the client and the teams were aligned that the process could move forward.

Arshad took away several key learnings:

Perspective. Continual learning is a mindset. We are all entrenched in our day-to-day activities and executing a multitude of tasks. It is critical to step back, reflect, and see these interactions from all sides.

Skills. None of us know all the answers. Even the best in any field need to find time to learn and grow. The time that we took to work on self-regulation, presence, and communication skills were critical elements in achieving collaboration with his client and the client's team.

Practice. Having the opportunity to try on the new behaviors in a safe learning environment was crucial. Colleagues can provide feedback and insights that are immediately useful. Being able to learn from and with each other makes a huge difference in daily performance in front of clients.

. . .

Expanding into conflict takes courage. It takes facing your fears and insecurities. It takes letting go of how you want someone else to feel or think. It demands that you show up with no distractions and engage fully with others. When you no longer feel tied to your point of view and are willing to hear and truly appreciate someone else's point of view, something miraculous happens. Defenses go down. People relax and let go of their positions, and the opportunity for true dialogue opens up. And that puts a smile on everyone's face.

5

THE ART OF DEVELOPING PHYSICAL AND VOCAL PRESENCE

Of all the things you wear, your expression is the most important.
—Janet Lane

D r. Paul Ekman found that even when people try to hide their emotions, they cannot. Their true emotions are revealed within 1/125 of a second in the form of micro expressions. Dr. Ekman posits that there are seven universal global emotions: anger, fear, sadness, disgust, surprise, contempt, and happiness. These are revealed through our facial expressions. Learning to become aware of our facial expressions and to read the expressions of others can enhance relationships and build empathy.

BUILDING EMOTIONAL AND EXPRESSIVE AWARENESS

One of my coaching clients, Roberto, is a successful plant manager and leader in Brazil. He engages with his workers regularly, walking the shop floor and speaking with them directly. Although they feel very close to him, he received feedback that many employees found it difficult to know what he thinks and feels. His wife would say to him, "Roberto, when you are happy your face is flat, when you are angry your face is flat, when you are sad your face is flat (Figure 5.1). Tell me, how do you really feel?"

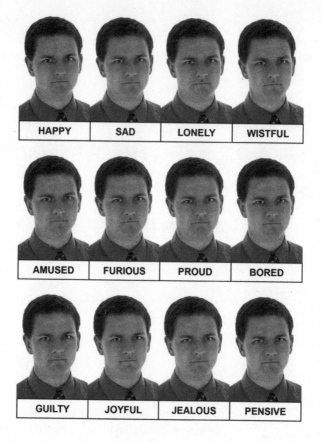

FIGURE 5.1 **Roberto's range of emotions**

Was Roberto incapable of expressing emotion? No, of course not. So, what was it that kept him from being more expressive at work? The only answer he could find was that he took his job seriously. He never considered that this would appear negative to others.

WHAT MESSAGE DO WE SEND WITHOUT SAYING A WORD?

As an actor and performing artist, I have worked for many years to understand how my emotions show up on my face and in my body. As a sales executive, I didn't think about how my emotions appeared. I would often find myself crunched for time and would walk around the office with a strained expression on my face.

It wasn't until I spoke with some folks in my office that I realized I was frowning. My expression communicated that I was very busy, so they tuned me out. I definitely did not want this to be my signature expression, and I realized that I had some work to do on myself.

Signature Expression

Are you aware of your facial expressions? Did you know that you have a signature expression? Let's try an experiment. Can you guess whose face is shown in Figure 5.2?

FIGURE 5.2 **Whose famous smile is this?**

If you guessed Stan Laurel, you are right. He was half of the famous silent comedy duo Laurel and Hardy. His face was his trademark. Even people unfamiliar with his work likely recognize this smile. When we watch Laurel, his expression seems perfectly natural, but it actually took many years to perfect. This is how powerful our facial expressions can become.

Look at the photos in Figure 5.3 and choose one of the pictures. Can you create that emotion on your face? Try a different one. Do this several times and see if you notice not just the large but the small changes in your face. How does each make you feel? Do you feel differently when you try on a particular expression?

FIGURE 5.3 **Practice trying on these emotions.**

Emotions are an important part of our ability to communicate. As Martha Alderson, a plot expert, said: "Emotions are universal, relatable and humanizing. Emotions always tell the truth."[1]

Many executives I work with are very cerebral. They reside more in their minds and their thoughts than in their bodies and emotions. But the more we are aware of our emotions and how they show up on our faces and the faces of others, the better we can respond appropriately and use them to influence and lead others more effectively.

PAUSE POINT

A disclaimer is important at this time. For folks who don't have strong narcissistic, sociopathic, or borderline tendencies, the notion that emotions always tell the truth holds true. Folks who tend toward or fully express these disorders can generate genuine emotion as a product of buying into their own lies and fabrications. It's why they tend to be fantastic manipulators; they defeat our emotional screening mechanisms. The issue of emotional deception does arise regularly in the workplace, especially as one moves up the ranks.

In order to be more effective as a leader, let's explore how we can influence ourselves to become more aware of the emotions that we hold and the expressions that we wear.

CULTIVATE A RESTING SMILE

Do we smile because we're happy, or are we happy because we smile? Many scientific studies have confirmed that parts of our bodies, mainly our faces, reinforce the feelings we are having. The reverse also seems to be true. Physical gestures and facial expressions can also influence how we actually feel. Our faces seem to communicate our states of mind not only to others but also to ourselves: "I smile, so I must be happy."[2]

Find a resting smile that suggests contentment, confidence, and generosity. As a way to discover the right expression, look at yourself in the mirror and experiment with different smiles. Try one that suggests overconfidence, maybe a wry smile, or even a goofy one. Find one that connects to your most generous and gracious inner self and make that your resting smile.

Try an Experiment

For one whole day, wear this resting smile and make note of how it feels. At the end of the day, answer the following questions.

When was it easy and natural to carry a resting smile?

_____

_____

_____

When was it difficult?

_____

_____

_____

Discovering Your Expressions

How can you become more aware of the various emotions and expressions that you carry on your face throughout your day? If you're having trouble thinking of ways that you might become more aware, try the following exercise.

Take a breath and make a choice. Whenever you find that you are wearing a negative emotion on your face, take a breath, relax, and let it drop away. Then, make a choice to switch to a positive feeling. What happens when you do this?

_____

_____

_____

EXPANDING PHYSICAL PRESENCE

If you are a parent of a child who is in ballet, like I am, you most likely have been to a *Nutcracker* performance or two. The *Nutcracker* is a yearly holiday tradition and a rite of passage for all young and professional dancers. It is a ballet that allows all ages to be involved in the performance. In one of the scenes there is a character called Mother Ginger. Mother Ginger is usually played by a man on stilts dressed like a matron with a huge skirt that can fit a dozen young *polichinelle* dancers (Figure 5.4). The part always garners a large reaction from the audience.

FIGURE 5.4 **Gerardo Interiano, Google's Head of External Affairs for the Southwest U.S., playing Mother Ginger at Ballet Austin**

Photo credit Christi Cuellar Lotz.

Two years ago, our daughter was in this particular scene playing one of the polichinelles. And don't you know, I was asked to be the Mother Ginger! I gladly accepted the part, mainly because I wanted the opportunity to be on stage with my daughter.

As parents, we watched the show a few times before it was my turn to play the part. The first Mother Ginger that we saw walked onto the stage and looked down at the floor the whole time, clearly very scared of falling. As an audience, we were scared for him as well. I personally felt my body tense up. The next night we saw a very different performer. He stood tall and confident as he stepped onto the stage. He exuded warmth and generosity as he waved his arms and greeted the entire audience. He was fun to watch. His physical presence and energy had an impact on us. He pulled us forward in our seats and got us to engage with him and the dancers. He also provided me with an image to keep in my mind, because I wanted to create the same experience for the audience.

The next day at a rehearsal, as I had been trained, I stood on my stilts in the middle of the stage (in street clothes) and looked out onto the empty 1,500-seat auditorium. I lifted my arms and consciously practiced expanding my presence into the entire space. I said the words, "I am present and open." I wanted every person to feel the same way I had felt the evening before, engaged, excited, and uplifted. By practicing, I created a sense memory that I could carry with me during the performance.

Present and Open

If you have the space and privacy, I encourage you to try this *Present and Open* exercise now. If not, find a private space where you can practice and experiment.

First, imagine standing on an empty stage facing out on a large auditorium. Lift your arms and say the words, "I am present and open." Imagine that you can reach every person in the theater with your presence.

Say the words again. How does this make you feel? What other words come to mind? Do you feel confident? Do you feel vulnerable, exposed, silly? Part of the process of expanding our presence is learning to become comfortable with feeling open and vulnerable. In my over 40 years in theater, this is one of my most essential learnings, and it is a key to executive presence—embodying both confidence and approachability. Find your way to be present and open.

LEAKS TO YOUR POWER

How often do we find ourselves crossing our arms, putting our hands in our pockets, fidgeting, or shifting onto the edges of our feet? We adopt these behaviors out of insecurity, judgment, boredom, and protection. Each of these are defensive gestures that I call leaks to your power. We all have them and we all do them, but we do need to fix them.

What are your leaks and habitual gestures?

_____
_____
_____
_____

What messages are these leaks and habitual gestures sending to others? "I'm insecure"? "I'm nervous"? "I'm unprepared"? "I'm out of my depth"?

_____
_____
_____
_____

What is the message that you would like to send?

_____
_____
_____
_____

What changes can you make to send this message?

_____
_____
_____
_____

It takes focus and attention to begin to shed these detractors of our executive poise and presence.

Try the *Present and Open* exercise again, this time start with the *Breathe-Connect-Land* sequence that we practiced earlier. As you lift your arms breathe in, then, in your mind, choose to expand your presence. Try it again using *Breathe-Expand-Land.* Remember, when you consciously tell yourself to expand you will begin to cultivate a spirit of openness and generosity.

WHEN YOU BREATHE, YOUR AUDIENCE BREATHES WITH YOU

This is an essential principle in theater. When you are about to step onto a stage or in front of a group, take a second to pause and take a breath, then smile, connect, breathe out, and land with the people that you will be speaking to. Let them take you in. If you try this in smaller groups, you might begin to notice a number of people take a breath with you. This is an important concept to understand. It is based on a psychological term first coined by neuroscientist Giacomo Rizzolatti: mirror neurons. These are a type of brain cell that respond equally when we perform an action and when we witness someone else perform the same action. It shows up as a gut-level reaction to other people's actions. It is how we understand, immediately and instinctively, others' thoughts, feelings, and intentions.

By taking a breath before you speak, you will relax and focus yourself. In turn, your audience will take a breath, relax, and focus with you.

This is precisely what conductors do with their orchestras. Picture for a moment that you are at a symphony concert sitting in the audience before the program listening to the players warm up. The orchestra leader steps onto her podium and taps her baton to gather the attention of her players. The players in turn focus their attention on her, and then in unison, the moment before they start to play, they take a collective breath. This is how orchestras get in sync with each other, and it's a powerful way for you to get in sync with your audience as well.

MAKE AN ENTRANCE

Master performers spend a good amount of time teaching their students how to make an entrance. There is an excellent scene in the movie *The Walk* about the famous wire walker Philippe Petit. Petit is speaking with a master wire walker who instructs him on how to make his entrance into the circus ring. He encourages Petit to walk slowly, pause, look at the audience, breathe, and let the audience "take you in." Don't do anything, he commands Petit, stand in your power, hold the moment, hold the space, hold their attention. It will always seem longer than you think, so take your time. Fill the moment with your confidence.

When I teach my executive presence program, I ask participants to stand in a circle. We take turns walking to an open spot in the circle and practice the sequence. It goes like this:

Walk to the open spot in the circle. Come to stillness, take a moment to breathe-connect-and-land inside of yourself. Then lift your eyes and connect with a few people in the circle. Slowly lift your arms and breathe in, connect with the others, and say the words, "I am present and open." Let your arms down slowly, take a beat, and walk back to your spot.

This sequence might seem simplistic (and maybe even a bit "out there"), but it's much more effective than you might originally think. This exercise demands that you be fully neutral and let go of any self-limiting thoughts or judgments. If you practice this sequence, you will begin to become much more aware and capable of landing and expanding in the most stressful of situations.

Try an Experiment

The next time you are in your office environment or are about to step into a meeting room, make a conscious choice to be present and open. Actually say the words to yourself: "I am present and open." Notice the impact that you have on others when you are in this state of mind.

Describe how people respond to you when you practice being present and open.

_____

_____

_____

Describe how people respond to you when you are distracted and closed.

_____

_____

_____

Once you become aware of yourself in these moments of distraction, you have created a space to make a conscious choice to do something different.

SIGNATURE STANCE

Many of our modern theater techniques originated from early Italian *commedia dell'arte*. This style of theater was employed by small troupes that traveled the countryside putting on plays. The characters were well known and loved by everyone. Each of the characters had a *Signature Stance* and movement that the actors would need to learn to correctly play the part as shown in Figure 5.5.

FIGURE 5.5 **An example of a *Signature Stance***
from early Italian *commedia dell'arte*

Let's use this theater technique to learn how to embody a strong *Signature Stance*. Think about a variety of familiar characters that exhibit a confident physical presence. For example:

- A ringmaster
- A ballerina
- A martial artist

For this exercise, read through this section and find a private space to experiment for about 15 minutes. Choose one of the characters above and think about their energy, how they hold themselves, and their physical bearing and poise. Begin to feel what it is like to stand and walk like this person. How does this person sit in a chair? Pretend you're walking out onto a stage to accept your Olympic medal, make an entrance, or take your final bow. Try on the character's *Signature Stance*.

This will feel stiff, uncomfortable, and awkward at first. Just relax, take a breath, and remember no one is watching. Figures 5.6 through 5.8 are a few images that you can use to jump-start this process. Give each one a few words that will guide your practice. For example:

FIGURE 5.6 **Ringmaster's *Signature Stance* to build command presence**

FIGURE 5.7 ***Signature Stances* in ballet training
to build posture, grace, and elegance**

FIGURE 5.8 **Martial artist *Signature Stance***
to get grounded and build confidence

- A ringmaster is confident, proud, and welcoming.
- A ballerina is elegant, graceful, and strong.
- A martial artist is grounded, fluid, and dangerous.

If you do not see someone on this list that resonates with you, find a character that does. Think of someone who exhibits this type of confidence and look for photographs that illustrate this person's physical presence and demeanor.

After you have done this, take some time for reflection. Consider the amount of training each of these people must have had to go through to become who they are. How much trial and error, repetition, and failure do you think they faced? Consider the amount of determination, resilience, and desire it took to get them to where they are today. Do you think they had a strong support system?

No matter who you choose, what makes these characters extraordinary is that when they show up, they take all of their training and self-confidence with them. They show up as their Best Self. The trick here is to borrow a bit of their presence, internalize it, and make it your own.

POWER OF VISUALIZATION

Visualization is an effective tool for preparing for critical situations. Take five minutes and find a quiet place to sit. Take a few deep breaths and connect with the image of your *Signature Stance*. Allow the image to influence your posture and feelings of confidence. Image yourself stepping into a meeting or onto a stage as a way to pattern your new behavior.

Visualization is a technique that professionals from various industries use as a tool for success. Golfers will tell you that as early as age 12 or 13, they imagined themselves on the eighteenth hole making a putt to win the US Open. Broadway actors remember back in high school when they would imagine themselves taking a bow at the end of their first Broadway performance.

Visualizing yourself achieving your goals is not just a silly game that you play as a child. Instead, it is a powerful enactment that can actually simulate reality. Brain science has proven that our minds cannot distinguish between the two experiences, so our success really depends on our personal commitment and attention to the activity in which we want to succeed.

FIND YOUR SPARK

In a recent program I worked with a Dutch engineer. He came to my session in Rotterdam aiming to become a better leader and communicator. He shared with me that his kids go to circus school and he volunteers there a lot. I asked him what he liked about the experience. As he explained how he loved the spirit of the circus performers, a wide and enthusiastic expression spread across his face. He literally came alive! The next day in the program, when he was about to give a presentation, I reminded him of our conversation and the expression that he had on his face. This immediately clicked with him, and he used it as a sense memory to give him a spark. It totally changed his presence, how he engaged with the group, and how he brought his message to life. It also changed how the group engaged with him. A week after the session he wrote me a note saying that this was the most memorable part of the session, and that he has used it several times as a positive trigger to unlock his energy and expressiveness.

Think about this for yourself. What is that one key, *your spark*, that unlocks your natural expressiveness, energy, and joy? Is it a memory, an image, or a physical stance?

EXPANDING VOCAL PRESENCE

Actors and performers not only learn to develop their energy and physical presence but they are also taught to expand their vocal range, expressiveness, and power. Why? Because we want our words to matter. Actors and performers want their words to reach their intended target and have impact.

This should be no different in our roles as business leaders. Yet, how often do we hear the monotoned drone of uninspired speeches and day-to-day meetings filled with technobabble, acronyms, and corporate jargon? All too often.

The good news is this: given the backdrop of bland, characterless, and unimaginative voices in our working lives, you have the opportunity to stand out. You have a wide-open palette upon which you can create lasting and memorable impressions in the ears of those whom you hope to influence. All it takes is an understanding of the variables involved, an awareness of the impact of your voice, a desire to improve, and a little practice.

Understanding the Voice

As I mentioned above, the most common pattern that we hear in business is a monotone voice. This is a voice that is devoid of variety, tone, expression, and meaning. When we hear a monotone voice, we feel a sense of disengagement. (And most of the time a monotone voice is accompanied by an equally flat emotional, physical, and facial expression.)

The tone of one's voice holds energy and attitude. We derive instantaneous meaning from the tone of someone's voice.

Let's go through some of the most recognizable tones:

- **Monotone**—a voice devoid of variety, emotion, and meaning.
- **Aggressive**—a sharp and jarring voice that creates distress.
- **Commanding**—a bellowing voice that captures immediate attention.
- **Inviting**—a melodic voice that draws the listener in.
- **Questioning**—a voice that goes up at the end of a sentence. Most people understand how to use a questioning tone. This is different from the

vocal phenomenon called upspeak, which is when you turn statements into questions as a result of inflection. It can be a sign of deference and insecurity and can undercut your credibility. Avoid this at all costs.

- **Rousing**—a voice that makes the listener stand up and cheer.
- **Demeaning**—a voice that makes the listener cower.

Our voices also hold a certain cadence and intonation that underscore the meanings behind our messages. These include the following:

- **Staccato**—a short, clipped pattern of speech.
- **Legato**—a smooth and connected pattern of speech.

The following are variables with which we can become familiar to enhance our tone and cadence.

- **Pitch**—high to low.
- **Pace**—fast to slow.
- **Volume**—loud to soft.
- **Quality**—clear, gravely, vocal fry. For vocal fry, think of the Wicked Witch of the West in the Wizard of Oz. It can undercut your credibility.
- **Resonance**—think of Darth Vader in *Star Wars*.
- **Articulation**—think of the crisp voices of the British.
- **Breath**—the foundation upon which all great voices are built.

BRINGING WORDS TO LIFE

Whenever actors or performers are presented with a text, they do an initial reading. This is an opportunity to *taste* the words as they are spoken and to begin to discover a natural cadence and rhythm.

Let's use a sample text from Shakespeare. The words from Shakespeare tend to be dense phrases that demand precision, timing, and breath. The words below are those of Polonius, the chief counselor of the king in *Hamlet*. He is described as a windbag and rambler of wisdom, and he says these words to his son to guide him. Take a moment now and say these words out loud.

> This above all, to thine own self be true, And it must follow, as the night the day, Thou canst not then be false to any man.[3]

How did you do? In the hundreds of times that I have introduced this exercise in my classes, very few people take a breath before or at any time in the course of saying these words. Let's practice.

Breathing: A Matter of Training

Upon a first reading, actors are trained to look for natural pause points and then score the script in those places where they will take a breath. It would look like this:

> This above all, to thine own self be true, /And it must follow, as the night the day. /Thou canst not then be false to any man.

Now, try again. This time take a breath first, then say the entire first line. Speak the words out as you breathe out. Then, take another breath in and speak out the second line and then the third line in the same manner.

If you like, you can visit my website for a short video where I walk you through this exercise. I have had many executives say that this is one of the most important skills that they take away with them from my sessions. You might ask, why? A close friend describes it this way:

> Before going into an important meeting, I make sure to get in touch with my breathing. I want to be sure that I am comfortable and not too eager to get my point across first. I want to feel settled and present.
>
> When I am in the moment with my client, I am aware of my breathing patterns and allow myself to breathe, speak, and then pause. This has had a profound impact on how my client pays attention to my words. It also gives them the time to process what I have said before I introduce my next thought or idea.

Resonance

Think of a TV news anchor. An anchor's voice can be described as having resonance, gravitas, and the weight of authority. Resonance adds depth, projects confidence, and is important for anyone to learn as soon as possible in his or her career.

It begins with a yawn.

Try it now. Make yourself yawn and breathe in. Then say the words from Shakespeare as you breathe out. Repeat. Repeat. Repeat.

Now, experiment with the words and phrases below that you can try to help you deepen your voice.

- **"How wide the sky."** Open your arms as you say the words. Exaggerate the opening and closing of your mouth. When you say the word *wide*, make sure to open your mouth wide and show your teeth.

- **"Luke, I am your Father."** (Pronounced "Faaather," of course.) This is my personal favorite. Stretch out each word. Have fun with it.

Articulation

There is an expression, "If you are not spitting, it's not Shakespeare."

Articulating our words, carving out each syllable, and over-enunciating is the key to clear speech.

Play Polonius again. Spit the words out. Get explosive! Now, say them again. This time over-*articulate* the closing consonants at the end of each word.

The Art of Practice

You know the story: a woman gets out of a cab on 57th Street in New York City and sees a man carrying a violin. She stops him and asks in a hurried voice, "How do you get to Carnegie Hall?" Without missing a beat, the man replies, "Practice!"

The first step in the artist's journey is when he or she discovers the value of discipline. With discipline comes mastery.

I recommend writing the words spoken by Polonius in *Hamlet* as well as experimenting with the cadence and intonation included in this chapter. Practice them wherever you can—in the car ride to the office, when you brush your hair, or before you go to bed.

You can also practice with a peer or record yourself on your phone. The more you practice, the more you will start to hear the little things in both your own voice and others' as well.

THE ACTOR'S SECRET

Have you ever been to a Broadway show and been thrilled by a particular performance? As you were walking out of the theater, have you ever wondered how someone can bring that level of energy, focus, and honesty to her performance every single night? One of the most powerful ideas is called the actor's "secret." In order to keep your performance fresh, you always need to be working on something. This could be a quality of your voice or a physical mannerism. It could be the way you deliver a line that surprises your scene partner. The question is, what are you secretly working on for the day?

Theatrical Monologues

If you are interested in taking this to the next level, I recommend doing a web search on the best theater monologues. You will discover a wealth of resources at your fingertips.

One of my coaching clients mentioned that the vice president in her department had an amazing presence. He stood tall, poised, and confident. He also had a strong yet flexible voice. She always thought he must have been naturally gifted. One day they were in a conversation and this topic came up. He said that, as an introvert, he had always felt awkward in social situations. He knew that if he wanted to advance he needed to address this discomfort. As a result, he enrolled in a weekly theater class for over a year, which enabled him to transform his presence and helped him in his career.

So, what do you want to work on? Decide and start practicing.

THE ART OF
TRANSITIONING

We do on stage things that are supposed to happen off.
Which is a kind of integrity, if you look on every exit
as being an entrance somewhere else.
—TOM STOPPARD,
Rosencrantz and Guildenstern Are Dead

One of the dilemmas of work and life is the sheer number of tasks that need to get done in a day. Moreover, it appears the more technology introduced to help us get all these things done, the more distracted we become. Learning to navigate transitions in both our work and personal lives is precisely a place where, if we put our attention, we can greatly increase the quality of our relationships, effectiveness, and overall contributions.

In this chapter we are going to look at two of the most important types of transitions:

1. The *small* transitions that we make in our day-to-day interactions and activities.

2. The *large* transitions that we make in our careers.

Both small and large transitions have internal and external aspects. Economist and leadership expert Herminia Ibarra explains as follows:

The external process is about developing a reputation for leadership potential and competency; it can dramatically change how we see ourselves. The internal process concerns the evolution of our own internal motivations and self-definition; it doesn't happen in a vacuum but rather in our relationships with others.[1]

Traditional leadership development tends to focus on internal shifts of awareness and thinking. As an executive coach I often see people struggle to translate this awareness into action. We have a proliferation of video courses that tell us who to be, what to think, and how to act. I was recently invited by Kevin Kruse to record a full-length course on his platform LEADx Academy titled, "Developing Your Executive Presence." One of my program participants noted that he consistently watched videos and read articles about developing executive presence. Those videos and articles certainly highlighted the importance of developing his executive presence—however, he did not see any changes in himself as a result of watching or reading.

This is precisely why a theater arts approach to leadership development is so powerful. Performing artists are taught to try on and experiment with behaviors to see how they feel to us. They are also encouraged to observe the reactions or responses their actions or behaviors elicit in others. We reflect on the feedback, decide what to keep and what to let go, and try again. This creates a refining process that deepens our self-awareness and gives us the ability to choose who we want to be and what we want to be known for. This is how artists develop and actualize their Best Self and how you can too.

DAILY TRANSITIONS

How often have you had one of those days where you found yourself going from meeting, to meeting, to meeting, to meeting, to meeting? Were you able to mentally "reset" before every meeting, or did you find yourself distracted in the next meeting—or longer? Were you able to bring your Best Self to each and every interaction during the day? Probably not.

Theater is about entrances and exits. The middle takes care of itself.
—ANONYMOUS

This quote was repeated many times during my theater training. At theater school we would experiment and practice all sorts of entrances, crosses, and exits on the stage until we became acutely aware of our presence, energy, and mannerisms. The purpose of these exercises was to build our sensitivity to the impact that we had on our audience, to access our creativity under stress, and to diminish our feelings of self-consciousness. We practiced and failed, and then tried again until we finally succeeded in doing something spontaneous and natural. The more we experimented (see "Trials by Fire" in Chapter 1), the more we honed our awareness, instincts, and timing.

Our days at work are filled with transitions. We are always moving from one thought to another, one space to another, one meeting to another. What would happen if we were to consider what Tom Stoppard suggests in this chapter's epigraph—that every exit we make is an entrance to somewhere else? What would this mentality begin to open for us?

I was asked by a local business owner in the Boston area if I could spend some time with his son to help him prepare for his eventual succession into leading the family business. The young man was bright, energetic, and full of ideas. His one big issue was that he operated at lightning speed.

One morning, after we had worked together for a month or so, I was sitting in a conference room waiting for Brent to show up for our session. It was about three minutes past the hour. Suddenly the door flew open, and all I could see was a streak as Brent sailed past me and landed in a chair across the table. In my mind I imagined papers flying up into the air like you see in the cartoons. I was startled. I smiled, looked at him in the eyes, and asked him if he would be willing to stand up, go back outside, close the door, and put into practice the routine that we had been working on.

The sequence is one you're familiar with by now—*Breathe-Connect-Land*—and one that you can put into practice immediately as well. Arrive at the door, pause, get still, and take a deep breath. Grab the handle and connect with the purpose of the meeting. As you breathe out, land inside of yourself with a feeling of confidence. Then, enter into the new space.

As soon as Brent stepped into the room, he paused, took another breath, then connected and landed with me. My whole experience of him changed. He now seemed to have cause and intention. He had a larger sense about him, and his presence increased. He seemed much more confident, open, and ready for our conversation.

What kind of an impression do you think you make in your office when you race from person to person and from meeting to meeting? How do you think people experienced you? How do others likely experience themselves when you are with them? What story might others tell when you're gone?

The way you navigate your work environment, the energy you embody when you interact with others, and the results that you get need to be assessed in order to find the answers to these questions. By focusing on the actual transition moments during your day, you will start to develop a greater awareness of the interactions you have with others.

Practice Transitioning

Imagine for a moment that you live in New York City and you are an actor in a Broadway show. You need to be at the theater by 2 p.m. It's about a 10-block walk to the theater. You had a difficult morning and start your short trek down 7th Avenue. The traffic is noisy and chaotic. Police sirens and truck horns fill the air. Your head is filled with the thoughts and emotions of your life. You reach Times Square and take a left onto 42nd Street.

You take a deep breath and notice the noise level decrease. You wave to a friend in the show, and it brings a smile to your face. You relax. You reach the theater and head to the stage door. Your pace slows and you can hear the sound of your footsteps echo against the brick walls. The rhythm of your breath begins to sync with the pace of your steps. The world becomes silent. You open the stage door and step over the threshold. The door closes, you leave the world behind, and you land in the theater. This is the art of transitioning.

EXITS AND ENTRANCES

In theater as in real life, transitions can be the focal point of anxiety and drama. As Shakespeare wrote so eloquently in *As You Like It*:

> *All the world's a stage,*
> *And all the men and women merely players;*
> *They have their exits and their entrances,*
> *And one man in his time plays many parts.*

How we prepare for these parts, and how we move efficiently, effectively, and elegantly from one scene to another and from one role to another is the discipline of acting. It is also the discipline of leading.

Develop a Yoga Mind

Let's use the discipline of yoga to help make this idea more tangible. Yoga is an ancient discipline that serves to integrate our minds, hearts, and bodies. Yoga can increase our physical strength, flexibility, and balance. It is also a powerful discipline for developing a clear and calm mind. Let's call it a Yoga Mind.

Much like the image I used above of walking to the theater, a Yoga Mind is cultivated through practice and is a resource at your service when you are confronted with or preparing for stressful and critical situations. The first step is *overcoming the internal resistance to change.*

Let's say we have to attend a yoga class that starts at 6:00 p.m. and it's only four blocks away from our office. It's 5:30 p.m. and our workday is ending. Even thinking about going to the class begins to create a bit of stress: Will we get there on time? Should I really be going to class when I have so much to do at home?

It's important to understand that moving from the analytical, working on spreadsheets and analyzing data, to the kinesthetic/emotional parts of ourselves, interacting with ourselves and others in a different way, *takes a transition step.*

This is where the Yoga Mind comes into play.

Rather than waiting until the last moment to get moving, take a few minutes (preferably 15 or more) to sit quietly in your chair and review your day. What went well? What needs your attention tonight or tomorrow? Write them down, take a breath, and let these go.

Now you put your attention to the yoga class and everything that will happen to get there. Picture leaving the office and getting to the studio. Imagine your body relaxing as you walk into the room. Feel the warmth, smell the incense, and hear the music. Picture all of this before you, then get up and recreate the experience for real.

How long does it take you to shake off your day before you can really settle down and land in this new space? For most people, the transition periods are about 20 minutes.

If you navigate them more gracefully you will be better able to engage fully with the task at hand.

Developing a Practice for Making Daily Transitions

Develop a simple transition practice:

- If someone comes into your office unexpectedly, take a second to stop what you were doing and focus on what you are now doing. Push your chair back, disengage from your work, turn and face the person, take a breath, and engage with him or her.

- When making a transition from tight focus analytical work to a critical conversation that requires empathy, take a moment and put the Yoga Mind into play. Look out of the window and notice the wind in the trees, feel the air, look at the people walking on the street, or just stand up and stretch. You might even watch a short one- or two-minute video that opens up your sense of connection and empathy.

- When you move from interacting with others and need to refocus on a spreadsheet or an important decision, do a simple math problem in your head. This can be done sitting in your chair or walking down the hall. My favorite is simply to double numbers. Start with two and two is four, four and four is eight, etc. It is easy to get started and then will take slightly more focus with each set. It will only take you 30 seconds but will help you make a better transition.

- First, understand the principles at play and then experiment to find your favorite tools to manage your transitions.

Challenge Your Preconceptions

It is very hard for all of us to leave our beliefs and judgments behind and enter into an experience with an open mind, or a beginner's mind. I first came upon this concept when I read *Zen Mind, Beginner's Mind* by Shunryu Suzuki in 1971. The book begins, "In the beginner's mind there are many possibilities, but in the expert's there are few."[2]

How does one cultivate this beginner's mindset? Let's apply this to your decision to take the lead on a major project. First, you need to do a bit of reflection before entering into a new situation.

- What do you want?
- What is your goal?
- What is your initial commitment to the activity?
- Can you suspend your judgment and be open to the experience?
- What would success look like in the first day? The first week? First month?

Think back to the apprentice model. You are currently at the novice stage, which is the most difficult and easiest to fall out of. What support systems can you put into place to ensure your success? Could you enlist a friend or colleague to join you? It is always better to have someone on the journey with you to help keep you motivated when things get tough.

MAKING THE TRANSITION
TO LEADING OTHERS

Research conducted by Development Dimensions International (DDI) revealed that "87 percent of first-time leaders feel frustrated, anxious and uncertain about their new role."[3] In another interactive study by Harris Poll, 69 percent of managers said that they experienced being uncomfortable with many types of employee communication.[4]

Why is transitioning from being an individual contributor to leading others so difficult? The reason is based solidly in brain science.

A number of studies have been conducted using the game of Tetris to demonstrate the difficulty of making mental transitions. In one, a professor at Harvard Medical School put a group of people in the basement of a building on campus and had them play Tetris for eight hours. The following week, one of the participants flagged down the professor on campus. "After your session," she said, "I went to the grocery store. Going down the aisle of cereal boxes I found myself impulsively rearranging the boxes on the shelf to see how they would fit together. What is up with that?"

This phenomenon is called attention density. What we repeatedly put our attention on builds an ingrained habit. And we tend to apply the principles of this habit to other parts of our lives—in other words, we do what we have trained our brains to do. It influences how we relate to others and how we see the world. So, when we move to a role where we lead others, we need to make a shift in where we put our attention. But this is where many of us get hung up.

One of the many ways in which our minds attempt to make life easier is to solve the first impression of the problem that it encounters. We see no more than we've been conditioned to see, based on our life experience, knowledge, and intelligence. In an attempt toward efficiency, our mind blocks clear vision and crowds out more critical information. This happens without any alarms sounding, so we never realize it is occurring.

Once we have settled on a point of view, we close off other lines of thought. Certain kinds of ideas occur to us, but only the kinds we are trained to see and no others.

Where this perception bias shows up most is in the quality of our listening. If we spend most of our days in problem-solving mode, our brains become wired to scan for problems. Our nervous systems also become conditioned to elicit positive hormones when we successfully find and solve a problem. It's no wonder that when someone comes into our office seeking guidance or with an issue, we jump right to problem-solving mode. Our ability to be fully present with that person and remain open until he has given us all of the facts is greatly hampered by our brain's conditioning to automatically look for and solve problems.

The late Chris Argyris created an excellent model called the "Ladder of Inference." It describes the thinking process that we go through, usually without realizing it, to get from a fact to a decision or action. The thinking stages can be seen as rungs on a ladder, with data at the bottom and assumptions, conclusions, beliefs, and actions at the top. When we are in execution mode, we quickly jump to conclusions based on limited data. Leaders need to learn how to slow down a bit and develop patience. Stay open, listen for the subtext, inquire, and ask questions before jumping to conclusions. It is important for us to become aware of our core biases and assumptions before we lock into any decision.

At any level, we need to make a transition in our minds on the amount of detail we offer as well. Audience matters here, and some general rules of thumb are:

- If you are speaking to a group of peers or people in your technical area, you are free to go into detail. They will appreciate it.

- If you are speaking up to senior leaders, give context and get to the point as quickly as you can. They will remember you for it.

Full-Scale Transition

Any transition into a more senior role or a new functional area or industry is a complex process involving a shift of all of the following:

- Mindset
- Role and identity
- Behaviors and actions

Let's take a look at what it means to make a complete transition of mindset, role, and identity, as well as actions and behaviors.

Accelerated Development

William was a cardiac surgeon who was also enrolled in the EMBA program at MIT. He said that at the same time he enrolled in the EMBA program, he had taken a new job at a hospital that split his duties in half, in the operating room (OR) and in overseeing the department. He said that he was getting tired of the grind in the OR, and because of that he wanted to expand into leadership.

William said that shifting from being a surgeon to a leader was a difficult transition. He had difficulty landing in his role. As a department overseer, it was not entirely his show anymore. People had difficulty relating to him, and he was not seen as approachable. People did not respond to him in the same way as they did when he was in the role of a surgeon. Things had changed.

Stories began circulating about him, and he couldn't get straight answers from his team.

He could not seem to get any traction on the ideas that he presented to his team, and he heard that people were actively blocking him.

After two months in his new position he received the feedback shown in Figure 6.1 from a system-wide survey.

Most Hated Physician

FIGURE 6.1 **Transitioning can be difficult**

To be clear, this wasn't a rogue comment from an employee with an axe to grind. This was systemic feedback. William was in shock. How could this be? When he worked as a surgeon, he would disregard such information, assign blame to the presenting party, and forge ahead. However, it was impossible to do this in his current situation. He knew he had a lot of work to do.

Fortunately, he was attending a leadership class at MIT at the same time. He learned how easily we become entrenched in our own perspectives, and in turn become oblivious to forces that affect business success.

He was introduced to the Three Lenses Framework for management success outlined in Figure 6.2. The *strategic lens* is that of the organizational architect. The architect designs strategies, processes, and procedures that fit the environment and facilitate the organization's objectives. Since much of William's prior experience was in the operating room, his strategic view and organizational processes were idiosyncratic and applicable to only the confines of his previous domain. He found it difficult to lift up his view and design strategies, processes, and procedures that fit his new environment.

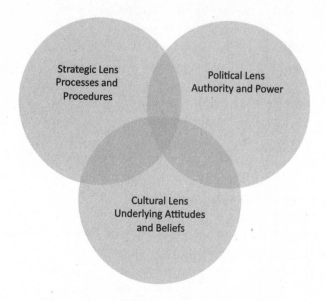

FIGURE 6.2 **MIT's Three Lenses Framework**

The *political lens* is that of the influencer and power player. The influencer navigates personal relationships and sees the organization as alliances, ambitions, and hierarchy. William realized that his sphere of influence and power centered mainly around the control of his personal environment. If he was going to be successful as a general manager and leader, it would be critical for him to understand subtler forms of influence. He needed to learn how to interact effectively with his peers and colleagues, as well as to give his direct reports a greater sense of ownership, to see the larger picture more clearly, and to feel a greater sense of team spirit.

Finally, the *cultural lens* is the realm of the storyteller. The storyteller operates in the world of norms, values, and artifacts used to create and communicate meaning and context. This is where William struggled the most and where his greatest leadership lessons were waiting for him.

William learned that in order to be a good manager, one must embrace all three of these spheres.

As he explored the model and the approach that he took to his work, he went back to his core training in medical school. It had been drilled into him to "Get it right, and get it right the first time, otherwise people could die!" This is a critical mindset for a cardiac surgeon. Surgeons literally hold people's lives in their hands. At the end of the day, it is the surgeon who is ultimately held accountable for any success or failure. It is no wonder surgeons have a reputation for arrogance. They would not be able to do their jobs without it.

William was used to sending a clear message to everyone: "This is my operating room. My anesthesiologist, my instruments, my nurse, my way or the highway!" He operated from a position of power and authority first. All processes and procedures were aligned accordingly. He never once considered the underlying attitudes and beliefs that held this system together because he never had to.

He quickly realized that his previous experiences had not prepared him for a wider leadership role, and if he truly wanted to be a leader, it was he who needed to change.

The first step for William was to do some inner focus work. He needed to reflect deeply on his mindset. His "my way or the highway" approach was definitely not working.

His sense of role and identity also needed to change. As a surgeon, he was the person with all of the answers. He was the one everyone else waited for—to make a decision, to choose the path, and even to order lunch.

In his new role, he didn't need to have "all the answers." Many of the very smart people who also worked on the floor might know more and have better solutions to the myriad of problems they faced every day. This is where the model of the Three Lenses came into view. He needed to step into the role of the cultural leader. He needed to get the pulse of his people. He needed to understand how decisions were made and how things got done. He needed to listen for the underlying narratives, attitudes, and beliefs and get in sync. He started to ask himself: What's my role as a leader? How am I showing up? How am I relating to others?

After much observation, asking for feedback, and giving of apologies, William slowly began to open up. He began to walk the floor, he talked to his staff, and he engaged in the exchange of ideas. He shared his questions and concerns, and his team began to see him as a real person.

In only six months, he achieved what originally had seemed impossible. Feedback from the system-wide survey now read as shown in Figure 6.3. William had turned his feedback around. The people in his organization truly appreciated the honest effort that he demonstrated, and it paid off.

Most Admired Physician

FIGURE 6.3 **Self-examination and honest effort will lead to successful transitioning.**

For William this process meant:

- **A shift in mindset.** From intellectual superiority to intellectual humility, and from having all of the answers to drawing out the collective intelligence of his team.

- **A shift in role and identity.** From the political lens of commander and authoritarian to the cultural lens of a coach, facilitator, and meaning maker.

- **A shift in actions and behavior.** He began to delegate and empower. He created stretch assignments to engage his team. He began to facilitate, inquire, and involve others. And he started to invest in developmental conversations with his team.

Developing a Plan for Making Larger Transitions

If you are in the process of making a full-scale transition, you can use the Three Lenses Framework to help you develop a plan of action.

Let's work on one together now.

Strategic Lens

Rather than making a huge entrance as you arrive in your new position, take a subtler approach. Begin by learning all you can about your new role and responsibilities. Invite your team into a conversation about which processes work well and which do not. Leverage the knowledge and experience of your new team to generate ideas and develop a plan together.

Expand into the strategic lens by answering the following:

- How does the work of your group support the goals of the organization?
- How do the current strategies, processes, and procedures integrate with other work groups?
- What improvements would help to enhance the operational experience?

Political Lens

Begin by observing the political power structures within your department and larger organization. Sit quietly in meetings; be alert and observe the flow of the dialogue. Watch for body language, vocal tones, and other communication clues. Expand into the political lens by answering the following:

- Who holds the knowledge in the organization?
- Who holds onto the positional power?
- How are decisions really made?

Cultural Lens

Adopt the mindset of an anthropologist and seek out the motives and values of the organization. Expand into the cultural lens by answering the following:

- What stories can you unearth about your team and the larger organization?
- Does the organization have a sense of humor?
- Is it a safe place for people to express their ideas?

. . .

Once you have begun to develop a sense for the people, environment, and systems within the organization, you can begin to think about the personal adjustments you might need to make to be successful. What is the mindset you will need to adopt? What is the most important role you can play to help your new team or organization achieve its strategic goals? What do you need to stop doing?

No matter the answers to these questions, it's crucial that you remember your presence has a huge impact on the people around you and your environment. A smile, a pause, and a positive observation can go a long way in paving your path to success.

THE ART OF
SELF-DISCOVERY AND
AUTHENTICITY

Being authentic can be defined as unquestionable congruent living,
the moment to moment alignment of your sincere thoughts,
values, emotions and actions.

—ANISA AVEN

Executives often ask me, "Rob, you were an actor and performer. Wasn't it your job to 'fake it' for a living?" Their wariness is understandable. Everyone in his or her working life has encountered one fake or another—and few would care to repeat the experience or be fake themselves. Yet over the course of this book, we've explored how you can incorporate aspects of acting and performance into how you present yourself to others. On the surface, this can seem like "faking it."

Anna Yusim, a psychiatrist who lives in New York City and works with many actors, addresses the discomfort between "performance" and "authenticity" very well:

In many ways, "performing" and "authenticity" are two opposite and often contradictory terms. A good performer is well-trained in the art of wearing different masks, whereas authenticity entails the removal of masks to discover who you are deep inside. Performing is discovering and taking on the truth of another person or situation, while authenticity involves being honest with yourself and living in your own truth.[1]

This is the central art of the actor, to bring a sense of authenticity to the role that he or she plays. Doesn't this hold true for executives as well? Aren't we just playing a role at work? If that's the case, how can we bring a sense of authenticity to our role as boss, colleague, and trusted employee? Yusim continues to impress upon us the importance of cultivating authenticity when playing a role:

> It's my belief that cultivating authenticity in one's life is a necessary pre-requisite not only for being a stellar performer, but also for living a fulfilled life. Perhaps the comparison to be made is "performer" verses "authentic artist." One approach is surface level while the latter is an evolved expression of the self and art.[2]

Yusim's distinction between a "performer" and an "authentic artist" is a worthy one, and the goal of this book is to help you become the latter. In this chapter, we will explore the concept of authenticity and introduce a process of self-discovery as the path toward creating a solid foundation for your own authentic leadership.

LEADER AS ARTIST

Think back to the story that I told of the executive from Ernst & Young who stepped up in front of his entire team and shared a struggle he was having. In this moment he challenged the very identity—the mask—that he had been building for over 20 years. By creating this mask for himself, he was in a way being a "performer" and not being an "authentic artist" as Yusim suggests. He dressed, walked, and spoke the part, but deep inside, this was not the real him. It was like he trying to be the person that others expected him to be, rather than the person he truly was.

Yusim adds an eloquent challenge to our quest toward being authentic by quoting e.e. cummings:

> "To be nobody but myself, in a world which is doing its best, night and day, to make me somebody else, means to fight the hardest

battle any human can fight, and never stop fighting." Aligning with authenticity in your daily life is a choice you make minute-by-minute, day-by-day.[3]

PAY NO ATTENTION TO THE MAN BEHIND THE CURTAIN

Let's use the movie *The Wizard of Oz* as way to explore this topic of authenticity. The wizard billed himself as the "Great and Powerful," so Dorothy and her friends went to him for answers to their questions. The first time they visited him, he sent them away on individual quests. He said that once they completed their goals, they could come back to him and he would grant their requests.

There is a great scene near the end of the movie where Dorothy and her friends revisit the wizard after completing their assigned tasks. The wizard is not keen to see them. Dorothy protests, explaining that they have done everything the wizard has asked and she just wants him to keep his promises. He keeps pushing them off until the curtain is pulled back by Toto, Dorothy's little dog. The curtain reveals a person like you or me. This wizard is a great showman, but he lacks the inner dimensions of character and true leadership.

It is critical for leaders to know what they are good at, what they want, what they stand for, and what they want to be known for. It is perfectly acceptable for a leader to have a bit of a showman in him or her, but there needs to be an equal amount (or more) of humility, vulnerability, and transparency to balance the equation.

The Search for Congruency

Back in Chapter 2 we discussed the concept of congruence as a state of mind when your real self is aligned with your ideal self. We experience distress when we try to be something that is not aligned with our real selves. This is clearly what the Wizard of Oz was experiencing. He was quite uncomfortable in the role he was playing as the Great and Powerful Oz. It was this discomfort that made him create a veneer of invincibility and exhibit the behavior of a bully.

Once the curtain was literally pulled back, he could no longer carry on the charade. It was only after the veneer was dropped and he shared his story that he was able to be honest with himself about what he wanted and what he needed to do. Similarly, it's only when we hear others' stories that we are able to fully understand and feel compassion for them.

Your Story Matters

Noel M. Tichy, a professor at the University of Michigan Business School and the coauthor of *The Cycle of Leadership*, points out that "every experience in our lives has value and a 'Teachable Point of View.' The very act of creating a Teachable Point of View makes people better leaders. Leaders come to understand the underlying assumptions that they hold about themselves, their organization, and business in general."[4]

In previous chapters, we've reflected upon the times when we were in our Best Self. These experiences build self-confidence and self-efficacy because they often involve overcoming large obstacles that require us to reach down deep and discover qualities and untested parts of ourselves. These moments build resilience.

Warren Bennis, a pioneer in the field of leadership development, wrote in his *Harvard Business Review* article "Crucible of Leadership" that one of the most reliable indicators and predictors of true leadership is an individual's ability to find meaning in negative events and to learn from even the most trying circumstances.[5] Put another way, the skills required to conquer adversity and emerge stronger and more committed are the same ones that make for extraordinary leaders. A crucible is, by definition, a transformative experience through which an individual comes to a new or an altered sense of identity.

MULTIPLE IDENTITIES

Authenticity is the process of connecting with our own sense of self and identity. Many of us have been taught to keep various parts of ourselves private and separate. More than a few senior executives believe that who they are and what they do or did in their private or prior lives has no place or meaning in their current roles at work. How this manifests is different for everyone.

Disconnected identities can happen when individuals rise to positions of authority. A transformation of sorts can occur where they begin to take themselves and the role they are about to inhabit very seriously. They appear to adopt a singular and rigid identity—and a whole new persona.

When leaders rely on their positional power to inflict punishment on their offenders, the negative repercussions on the existing relationships and culture can be devastating. Caustic environments are caused by caustic people. It is also important to realize that top leaders who tolerate these less-than-desirable behaviors are complicit in the behaviors and primarily responsible for creating these environments.

Authenticity starts with truly knowing who you are, where you come from, and what you stand for. Consider the following statements:

> I am the son of a black man from Kenya and a white woman from Kansas. I was raised with the help of a white grandfather . . . and a white grandmother . . . I've gone to some of the best schools in America and lived in one of the world's poorest nations. I am married to a black American who carries within her the blood of slaves and slave-owners—an inheritance we pass on to our two precious daughters . . . . [This] story . . . has seared into my genetic makeup the idea that this nation is more than the sum of its parts—that out of many, we are truly one.
>
> Barack Obama, President,
> United States of America

> My parents, my husband and my children have a lot to do with who I am. . . . Employees need to be able to bring their whole selves to work. . . . Even the CEO has to bring her whole self to work.
>
> Indra Nooyi, Chairman & CEO, PepsiCo[6]

The definition of oneself is complex and multifaceted. A person can have many identities, or self-definitions, based on attributes such as profession, gender, ethnicity, religion, nationality, and family roles. But how do our multiple identities shape our actions in organizations? The above quotes suggest that for leaders such as President Barack Obama and PepsiCo Chairman and CEO Indra Nooyi, their multiple identities are defining factors in who they are and what they do. For Obama, recognizing and reconciling his own multiple identities was a core part of how he connected with and led a pluralistic community. For Nooyi, bringing her whole self to work was one of the key ways in which she made a positive impact on her organization. Multiple identities are critical to people's lives, to those they work with, and to their organizations.

BE A STORY ARCHEOLOGIST

Taking the time to reflect upon your personal journey is a clear path toward discovering your many identities and forming an integrated sense of self. Think of it like conducting your own personal archeological dig. As a story archeologist, you search for deep narratives within your personal history and then mine for and unearth your most powerful stories. Contained within your stories are the clues to the values and principles that are most important to you and that describe you at your best. These stories serve to illustrate the challenges you have experienced in your life, how you faced these challenges, and the lessons that you learned. They also serve as an indisputable window into your core identity and validation of principles that underscore your leadership.

Before we can begin to look ahead at the next chapter in our life, we must become deeply familiar with who we were in our prior (and present) chapters.

Take some time to reflect upon and answer the questions below. Look for memorable moments or scenes in each chapters of your life. You might think about a time when you faced a choice and none of the options were ideal, when you took a stand for someone else, or when you challenged your boundaries.

These are the decision points, transitions, and self-defining events that have brought you to where and who you are today. If you lean toward visual stimulation, pick up a piece of paper and draw out your journey within each of the sections we will explore below. Be sure to identify the people, places, and events, as well as the affirming and challenging moments for each. Head to my website (www.leadingfromyourbestself.com/resources) to find a diagram that can get you started.

Childhood (ages 0–12)

What is the name of this chapter of your life?

_____

_____

_____

What would the first two sentences of this chapter be?

_____

_____

_____

Who were you as a child?

_____

_____

_____

What role did you play in your family? How did this impact you?

_____

_____

_____

Did you have a nickname? If so, what was it? What is the story behind this?

_____

_____

_____

What were you known for at this time?

_____

_____

_____

What was your most admired trait?

_____

_____

_____

What was your least admired trait?

_____

_____

_____

Describe your experience of choosing teams on the playground. What role did you play? Was it enjoyable or painful?

_____

_____

_____

Who were the three most influential people for you during this time? Were they mentors, coaches, friends, and/or family?

_____

_____

_____

_____

_____

Identify three memorable moments or scenes from this time period.
Give each a headline.

_____

_____

_____

_____

_____

_____

On a separate piece of paper, write a short paragraph describing each of
these moments or scenes and include the following details:

- How old were you?

- Where were you?

- What were you thinking, feeling, and wanting at this time?

- Who was with you?

- What were they thinking, feeling, and wanting?

- What did you learn?

- How did this event impact you and the course of your life?

Youth and Adolescence (ages 12–24)

What is the name of this chapter?

_____

_____

What would the first two sentences of this chapter be?

_____

_____

Were you an insider or outsider among your peers? Explain.

_____

_____

What were you known for?

_____

_____

_____

What mattered most to you?

_____

_____

_____

Who were the three most influential people for you during this time?
Were they mentors, coaches, friends, and/or family?

_____

_____

_____

What was the biggest lesson that you learned?

_____

_____

_____

Describe a goal or idea of who/what you wanted to be.

_____

_____

_____

When did you challenge your limits or expand your boundaries?

_____

_____

_____

Identify three moments or scenes that define this time. Give each
a headline.

_____

_____

_____

_____

_____

On a separate piece of paper, write a short paragraph describing each of these stories. Again, include the following details:

- How old were you?
- Where were you?
- What were you thinking, feeling, and wanting at this time?
- Who was with you?
- What were they thinking, feeling, and wanting?
- What did you learn?
- How did this event impact you and the course of your life?

Adulthood (ages 24–35)

What is the name of this chapter?

_____

_____

_____

What would the first two sentences of this chapter be?

_____

_____

_____

When did you first "feel" like an adult?

_____

_____

_____

What were you known for?

_____

_____

_____

What mattered most to you?

_____

_____

_____

Who were the three most influential people for you during this time?
Were they mentors, coaches, friends, and/or family?

_____

_____

_____

What were the three most important lessons that you learned
during this time?

_____

_____

_____

What was the most important decision you made as a young adult?

_____

_____

_____

_____

_____

Identify three moments or scenes that define this time. Give each
a headline.

_____

_____

_____

_____

_____

_____

On a separate piece of paper, write a short paragraph describing each of
these stories. Be sure to include the following details:

- How old were you?
- Where were you?
- What were you thinking, feeling, and wanting at this time?
- Who was with you?
- What were they thinking, feeling, and wanting?
- What did you learn?
- How did this event impact you and the course of your life?

The Search Toward Integration

Was there a part of yourself that you had to leave behind in order to fully step into adulthood?

_____

_____

_____

Is this unfulfilled part of you still calling you? Do you need to reclaim it?

_____

_____

_____

THE NEXT CHAPTER IN YOUR LEADERSHIP JOURNEY

Building your personal story can be easier than you might think. The framework laid out in the following pages can be the template to write your next chapter.

But before we get there, you need to understand your role as the protagonist in your own story.

A protagonist is the main character of a story and the one with whom we build an emotional connection and whom we watch transform. A protagonist is also the driver of the action in a story, an advocate or champion of a particular cause or action.

You are the protagonist, catalyst, and main character of your own authentic story (both in real life and in the context of this exercise). It's important to note that this model assumes that everyone is the main character in his or her own story, and that we simultaneously play a supporting role in the stories of others. This is not a model of leadership as much as it is a journey of self-discovery. Being the protagonist of your own story is not about being the person with all the answers, i.e., "the hero," but understanding who you are, what you want, and learning how to be flexible and adaptable and resilient in the midst of change.

So, what are the steps in a protagonist's journey? Let's take a look.

1. **A protagonist is good at something.** Every main character has specific capabilities, strengths, and gifts that are a result of his or her individual experience.

2. **They want something.** Protagonists have a clear and explicit goal. They yearn for something greater.

3. **There is an obstacle in their way.** External or internal barriers prevent this person from getting what he or she wants.

4. **The protagonist must go through transformation.** The main character of a story must become something greater than he or she was before.

Let's look at each of these points and discover what is unique about you as a main character of your story.

1. WHAT ARE YOU GOOD AT?

Identify your adaptive qualities, leadership strengths, and core capabilities. Think back and consolidate the insights that you gathered from the prior reflection questions in this book. These include your Best Self insights, interviews with colleagues, and personal story reflections.

_____

_____

_____

_____

_____

_____

_____

_____

2. WHAT DO YOU WANT?

What are your personal aspirations? Include both short-term and long-term goals and be as specific as possible.

_____

_____

_____

Why are these personal goals so important?

_____

_____

_____

What are your professional aspirations? Include both short-term and long-term goals and be as specific as possible.

_____

_____

_____

Why are these professional goals so important?

_____

_____

_____

What capabilities do you need to fulfill these goals?

_____

_____

_____

What capabilities do you already possess to fulfill these goals?

_____

_____

_____

What capabilities do you need to develop to fulfill these goals?

_____

_____

_____

3. WHAT IS IN THE WAY OF YOU ACHIEVING YOUR GOALS?

In what ways are you limiting yourself and restricting your growth? These can include current beliefs, mindsets, and more.

_____

_____

_____

What assumptions might you be making about these barriers that need to be challenged?

_____

_____

_____

In what ways are other people or circumstances limiting you or restricting your growth?

_____

_____

_____

What assumptions might you be making about these barriers that need to be changed?

_____

_____

_____

4. WHAT IS THE TRANSFORMATION THAT YOU NEED TO GO THROUGH TO GET TO YOUR FINAL GOAL?

What are you most ready for but have not allowed yourself to achieve?

_____

_____

_____

What part of yourself that no longer serves you do you need to let go of?

_____

_____

_____

What would it be like to live a fulfilled life?

_____

_____

_____

Going Deeper

In order to truly understand what drives you as an individual, it is essential to dive even deeper into what you want and why you want it. Answer the following questions in order to gain clarity on what propels you to act.

What part of yourself most defines who you are but is not obvious to others?

_____

_____

_____

What are your external motivations (money, fame, position, reward, etc.)?

_____

_____

_____

What are your internal motivations (autonomy, learning, belonging, mastery, etc.)?

_____

_____

_____

What were your top three career values 10 years ago?

1. _____

2. _____

3. _____

What are your top three career values now?

1. _____

2. _____

3. _____

What do you see as your top three career values in 10 years?

1. _____

2. _____

3. _____

What were you known for 10 years ago?

_____

_____

_____

What are you known for now?

_____

_____

_____

What do you want to be known for in the future?

_____

_____

_____

What are you most passionate about?

_____

_____

_____

What activities bring you the most energy?

_____

_____

_____

What inspires you?

_____

_____

_____

In what activities or situations are you at your best?

_____

_____

_____

Describe a time in your life when you felt the greatest sense of meaning and purpose.

_____

_____

_____

How could you put your gifts and talents to the best and highest use?

_____

_____

_____

Explain your purpose in life, at work, and/or at play in one sentence.

_____

_____

_____

Your Leadership Point of View

What are the top three values or principles that guide your leadership?

1. _____

2. _____

3. _____

What stories from your life best illustrate each of these values or principles from any time period? Please describe three separate stories.

1. _____
   _____
   _____
   _____

2. _____
   _____
   _____
   _____

3. _____
   _____
   _____
   _____

What is the vision that you have for yourself as a leader?
Describe this in detail.

_____
_____
_____
_____
_____

Your Next Chapter

What will the name of this chapter be?

_____
_____
_____

What will the first two sentences of this chapter be?

_____

_____

_____

What is the shift that you have made or are making to fulfill the vision you have for your future self?

_____

_____

_____

On what principle will your future be built?

_____

_____

_____

What can you do right now that will accelerate your process and get you what you want and where you want to be?

_____

_____

_____

Who can you reach out to that will support you in your journey?

_____

_____

_____

Legacy

Put yourself into your brightest future. What are you most proud of?

_____

_____

_____

How will you be remembered?

_____

_____

_____

What is the story that others will tell about you when you are gone?

_____

_____

_____

Write an epitaph that will best describe the impact that you had in your life.

_____

_____

_____

I AM

My daughter Maya was enrolled in a Montessori School through fifth grade. She became quite good at bringing her experiences to life through writing. One of the exercises that her class used was called an "I AM poem." I use it in many of my executive development programs as a way to break out of linear thinking and create a possibility mindset.

A sample of Maya's poem is below. She wrote this at nine years old.

> _I am . . . Maya_
> _I am . . . observant_
> _I wonder . . . about people's decisions_
> _I hear . . . people chatting in agreement_
> _I see . . . an open door waiting for me to step inside_
> _I want . . . to hear more stories_
> _I am . . . Enchanted_
>
> _I pretend . . . to be in a magical world with endless possibilities_
> _I feel . . . healthy and strong_
> _I touch . . . a friend's hand so I won't be alone_
> _I worry . . . about the slightest detail_
> _I cry . . . alone behind the curtain_
> _I am . . . an artist_
>
> _I understand . . . that not everything is sparkling_
> _I say . . . there is a bright side to everything_
> _I dream . . . about my future and how it will turn out_
> _I try . . . to get along with people_
> _I hope . . . there is a train waiting for me at every stop_
> _I am . . . Maya_

Try it for yourself. It is not about being perfect. It will be different every time you do it. If you feel stuck, set the poem in context, such as "I am a coach." This can make the process much easier.

I AM

I am _____

I wonder _____

I hear _____

I see _____

I want _____

I am _____

I pretend _____

I feel _____

I touch _____

I worry _____

I cry _____

I am _____

I understand _____

I say _____

I dream _____

I try _____

I hope _____

I am _____

THE ART OF RELATING
AND CONNECTING

I define connection as the energy that exists between people when they feel seen, heard, and valued; when they can give and receive without judgment; and when they derive sustenance and strength from the relationship.
—BRENÉ BROWN

At our core, we all want to be seen for who we truly are, for our gifts and talents, and for the value that we bring. We all want an opportunity to put these to the best and highest use. When we feel seen by another person we feel safe to bring our Best Self forward. This is when we do our best work, when we have our best insights, and when our results far exceed expectations.

At the beginning of my performing career I tried very hard to make my audience pay attention to me. I wanted so badly to be good at what I was doing and be successful that I never took the time to understand the dynamics of the relationship between a performer and his or her audience. As someone whose performance style was based on audience participation, this was not a good thing. It wasn't until I started working with my theater director and coach, Bill Finlay, that I learned how to establish this connection.

Bill would encourage me to think about how I wanted to relate to and engage with my audience. He urged me to go beyond trying to impress them with my latest skills and ask, "What do I want my audience to feel or do?" and "What kind of atmosphere do I want to create?" Did I want them to sit or stand quietly until it was time to clap? Or, did I want to enlist them as fellow collaborators?

With focus and practice, I developed a relaxed and welcoming style that would invite my audience to play.

In this chapter we will explore the different levels on which we relate to others and how these levels either block or facilitate great results. We will discuss the foundations of trust and the secrets to connecting authentically with others. At the end of the chapter we will explore the notion of multiple identities and insights toward living an integrated life.

LEVELS OF RELATING

Have you ever worked for someone who truly "got" you? Someone who saw something in you and gave you the encouragement and support to grow? Describe how that person related to you and how your interactions made you feel.

_____

_____

_____

Have you ever worked for someone who did not "get" you? What words would you use to describe how that person related to you and how your interactions made you feel?

_____

_____

_____

If the purpose of this book is to become better equipped to lead from our Best Self—and, in turn, create environments that allow others to lead from their Best Self—then the key lies in the way we relate to each other. The challenge for all of us is how to be fully present, authentic and open to others in the midst of our busy lives and the need to get things done.

Unfortunately, much of the difficulty we face in bringing our authentic self to the table might stem from the painful exposure to less than authentic ways of relating. Authenticity is a practice requiring tremendous courage and skill. It begins with understanding that we all have positive and negative relational experiences, but the fundamental need to be understood remains at the core. We must first, and at all costs, protect ourselves and those around us. Only then can we develop the requisite interpersonal skills to create bridges of understanding, alignment, and momentum.

Because work is so execution-focused, when we get busy we can some-times jump right into the task to accomplish our goal. It is easy to forget that there are other people involved in the equation. Relating to each other is critical in improving the quality of our work and achieving our personal and professional goals.

Let's look at three basic levels of how we relate to each other in order to increase our overall effectiveness and contribution (Figure 8.1).

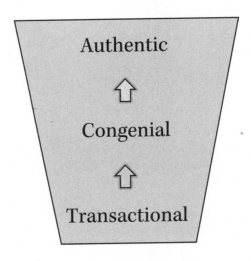

FIGURE 8.1 **The three levels of relating to others**

Level 1: Transactional Relationships

Like any transaction, this level of relating is a simple exchange, action, or activity involving two parties that reciprocally affect or influence each other. For example, if you were working in a hospital, there would be a variety of procedures, forms, and signatures that you would need to collect in a day. These transactions are critical to making sure that the process of patient intake and discharge goes smoothly and is trackable. We would never get things done if we did not conduct a myriad of transactions throughout our day.

The question is in how many of these interactions do you feel invisible or small, or leave less than satisfied and wanting more? How many of these relationships would you like to, or maybe even need to, be more than transactional? Let's flip the roles. In how many of these interactions are you the person who, by virtue of your higher status, simply looks through or dismisses the efforts of others?

Level 2: Congenial Relationships

We all have those relationships that are quite pleasant and cooperative. You might know and work with someone for years, maybe even have spent hours with them at the ball game or on the golf course but know nothing essential about that person. What happens when you need to move past the niceties and get to something real? Can you do it?

Level 3: Authentic Relationships

Authentic connection is based on shared values, trust, and the appreciation of someone's talents, capabilities, and limitations. When operating on this level, we lead with a sense of transparency, intimacy, and vulnerability, as well as with a deep respect for the differences that lay between each other. It also takes courage to relate to others in an authentic manner.

Making the Transition to a New Level of Relating

Learning to relate to others authentically has solid business implications. What happens when business demands that you begin interacting with members of the C-Suite in order to secure binding contracts? How do you encourage a higher level of engagement in a department that has a history of negativity? How can you build a relationship with a colleague whose cooperation is critical to your success?

Get to the Heart of the Matter, Right Away!

Picture this: you are a national sales manager of a commercial security company who has built great relationships with your clients. Unfortunately, negotiations are stuck and you need to break the stalemate. If only you could get the ear of the CEO. One afternoon you are walking out of the client's office and—what do you know!—you bump into the CEO on your way out. This is your big chance! He is friendly and you end up walking together for a few minutes. After you shake hands, you pause and feel a cringe of regret because the only topic that you could think of to talk with him about was football.

What would you do in this situation? What would you say? How would you connect with someone at a much higher level than you are used to relating to—and quickly? Do you just start talking about yourself without making a point? How do you break out of the awkwardness of the moment?

In most cases, the best rule of thumb is to stop talking about yourself and put your attention on the other person. Be curious and take a sincere interest in what is most important to him or her. Ask a question such as:

- What is most important to you in your role?

- What is the biggest challenge that you are currently facing?

- What are you most passionate about, or do you care about the most?

- What matters most to you in the way you like to see things done?

These questions will start a different type of conversation. They will demonstrate an authentic quality that engenders trust and will reveal your motives as less about appearing smart and more about truly caring for your client.

How would this play out in real business situations? Below are real stories from clients who have made the leap and got to the heart of the matter—when they never would have in the past!

Example #1: Lindsey

Lindsey is a portfolio manager in a financial services firm, and she's been asked to step into a meeting with an important and concerned client. The market is at a low point, and she's recommended that the client hold on to his current investments. The client has responded that he wants to sell and wants to talk with her directly. Lindsey walks into the meeting and immediately begins to pitch her point of view: buy low, sell high. The client looks at the account manager and, in frustration, calls an end to the meeting.

Can you see how this was a one-way transaction? What could Lindsey have done instead?

This is the type of situation where getting to the heart of the matter can help. Lean in, inquire, and ask powerful questions. In Lindsey's case, she could have said something along the lines of, "I can see that your desire to sell goes against conventional wisdom. Can I ask if there is something deeper behind your decision? Help us to understand, so that we can best serve you." How do you think this scenario would have played out if she had asked these questions instead of pushing her own agenda unknowingly?

Example #2: Dirk

I had been coaching Dirk, a senior manager at a global bank, and we were working on his executive presence. He was trying to be more relational with his staff. He told me that there was a person at the front desk and several more administrative people with whom he interacted daily. I asked Dirk the nature of his interactions, and he said that they were mostly transactional. I probed further and discovered that he didn't even know all of these people's names. We discussed what it meant to create a conducive and authentic work environment and the importance of employee experience at every level. We discussed how he could make a commitment to raising the level of relating with all members of his office staff. To achieve this, we discussed why it would be important and who would benefit from it. We also discussed the power of endorsements, catching employees doing something well, and acknowledging their efforts. When people feel seen and valued for their contribution, the quality of their work goes way up. After a couple of months, to his surprise and delight, this is exactly what happened.

How many of your daily interactions are solely transactional in nature? What is preventing you from elevating the way you relate to your clients, employees, colleagues, or senior leaders? What question could you ask that will go to the heart of the matter, will stay with them, and they will remember and appreciate you for?

Listen to Listen

Once you have been able to break through and ask a question that gets to the heart of the matter, the next thing to do is to listen. And I mean truly *listen to listen.*

Think about this for a moment: how often do we listen to speak, listen to solve the problem, or even half-listen to another person?

None of these methods will enhance your relationships. Besides, you might even miss the most important piece of information the other person is trying to communicate. It could be in the way the person is talking, his or her energy or body language, or a wistful sigh, but each of these are the signals that we receive when we are fully present and listening to listen.

Authentic connection relies upon the unquestionable quality of our presence, our listening skills, and our respect of another person's values, beliefs, and differences—in the moment, eyeball to eyeball. It is in the quality of our connection with others that we discover our own authenticity.

Authentic Connection—Well, Not Really

It was 4 p.m. on a Friday afternoon in the fall of 2008 and I was sitting at my desk finishing up an e-mail to a client. It was the end of a long and hard week, but a good one. I could smell the popcorn from down the hall and hear the laughter of my colleagues gathering in the break room. I knew there was a cold beer waiting for me.

Suddenly I felt a presence in the doorway. I looked up and saw my boss standing there. "Got a minute?"

"Sure," I said, and as I turned in my seat he came in and stood in front of me.

"How was your week?" he asked.

"Good, really good, actually," I said cautiously.

"Tell me about it?" he asked.

I softened up a bit and gave him a quick sketch of the highlights. Then, as I started to tell him a bit more about one particular win, I saw his face go blank and his eyes get tight. I stopped in midsentence and said, "That's not what you came here for, is it?"

"No," he replied. "What are the final numbers going to be for American Express and Harvard Business School?"

I referred to my spreadsheet that was open on my desktop, then turned back and gave him the numbers. Without a word of acknowledgment, he left.

I sat there dumbfounded and was left thinking, "Why didn't I see this coming?" I felt disappointed in myself for going into too much detail, as well as a bit frustrated with my boss. He could have just asked me for the numbers. He didn't need to feign interest in my week. Was this really the state of our relationship? What part did I play in this?

Establishing authentic and trusting relationships at work is not always easy. We constantly seek balance between driving our own agenda and pausing enough to make a genuine connection with someone else in the moment. Each of us is living our own, unique experience. We are all the main characters in our own life stories. As leaders, we need to learn how to truly relate and connect with others. We need to continually remind ourselves that to get the best out of others, they need to feel seen, heard, and valued. That their effort matters, that their story matters.

PUTTING THE PIECES TOGETHER

Let me tell you about how a client, Donny was able to quickly put his career on the fast track by utilizing all of the skills we have been discussing.

Donny was a brilliant engineer in a top European bank. He was leading a team of five direct reports and an organization of over 100 engineers. The focus of their work was the creation of a mobile technology platform for the bank. Unfortunately, he was struggling. In our initial conversation he said the following things: "Can I take that promotion without losing my soul?," "I just don't see myself as a leader," and "My leadership team is disengaged, what do I do?"

Can you relate to any of these questions or statements?

I was sitting in the lobby of a large corporate office in Amsterdam waiting to meet Donny for the first time. I had spoken to him on the phone, and we had built a good connection. I looked at every person who came in and out of the building. All very well dressed in professional attire. Then this guy walked in wearing blue jeans and a T-shirt. I immediately got an image in my mind of a sound tech for a rock band. What do you know, it was Donny!

Impressions Matter

Donny was clearly sending a message to his colleagues: "I'm my own person and I don't buy into the corporate culture." In our conversation, Donny had expressed his discomfort with "being a leader." He explained, "I love connecting with the engineers, and I enjoy walking the halls and talking with them about their work. I can relate to them much easier than to my peers and senior leaders."

He continued. "I see so many of my former peers go for the promotion and then become someone totally different," he said. "I don't want to be that person. I don't want to change who I am. I don't want to sell out."

Because of his experiences, values, and beliefs, Donny was struggling in a number of areas.

- First, he was unable to focus the efforts of his direct reports. They were disengaged and going in different directions.

- Second, he did not have a voice on the senior management team. They did not take him seriously.

- Third, he could not influence these senior leaders to see the brilliant solution he and his team had for mobile technology.

So where could Donny go from here? Could he go anywhere and still hold on to the things that were important to him? Together we explored his personal history. He'd started coding at the age of 11 and always kept up with the latest technology. Falling in line wasn't in his nature. His impulse was to challenge authority every chance he got. He did, however, have solid values of loyalty, honesty, and integrity.

The key to helping Donny was to get him to ask himself the right questions.

- How did he show up?
- What was the message he sent without saying a word?
- What was most important to him?
- What did his team want and need from him?

Everything clicked when I asked Donny if he knew what was most important to his team and if he had ever asked. He did not. Donny was a smart guy—he just had never asked himself these questions. He was stuck inside of his own perspective, and he needed to exercise empathy and be curious about what his team was thinking, feeling, and wanting.

At our next session he told me that he had pulled his team together and shared what was important to him and had asked what was important to them. He listened. It started a much deeper conversation. He was able to draw them together and get everyone aligned around a team vision and a sense of purpose.

If you lead a team, do what Donny did. At your next meeting:

- Share your intent to increase team effectiveness and trust.
- Let your team members know what is most important to you as a person and as a leader.
- Ask each of them to share something of personal and professional value and importance.

These activities will spark a deeper conversation with your team members, and they will take their cue from you and begin to share too!

Do I Really Belong?

As human beings we are always searching for a sense of community—a place where we fit in, where we feel safe, where our contribution matters and is appreciated, and where we develop a sense of identity. Many people find this sense of belonging outside of work, in families, faith communities, artistic communities, and the like. However, with more and more of our time being spent at work, the corporate organization now serves as the main community within which we operate. The issue with this is the nature of the arrangement. Money for work. Do we give our trust blindly to an organization? Do its leaders have our best interest in mind? Do they value and care about what is important to us? Can we trust them? Will we have to compromise our values in order to make it, or can we continue to lead from our authentic and Best Self? No matter where you stand in an organization, you can make a difference. You can elevate your way of relating to others immediately by encouraging the right behaviors, engaging in random acts of kindness, and expressing heartfelt words of appreciation.

RELATE RIGHT NOW!

You can start relating more authentically right away. Here is how:

- Make a list of your core relationships and daily interactions.
- How many of these relationships would you characterize as authentic? Why? What benefits do you gain from these relationships?
- Which would you characterize as congenial? Why?
- Which would you characterize as transactional? Why?
- How many of the transactional and congenial relationships would you like to or need to be more authentic?
- Follow this basic formula to build authentic connections:
    - Be curious.
    - Put your full attention on the other person.
    - Ask powerful questions that go to the heart of the matter.
    - Listen to listen.

THE ART OF STORY SHARING, STORYTELLING, AND MEANING MAKING

Great stories happen all around you every day.
At the time they're happening, you don't think of them as stories.
You probably don't think about them at all. You experience them.
You enjoy them. You learn from them. You're inspired by them.
They only become stories if someone is wise enough to share them.
That's when a story is born.

—PAUL SMITH

grew up in a family-run flower shop in the heart of the East Side of Providence, Rhode Island. Our family's business was located on Thayer Street, the main shopping and eating area serving Brown University. My grandfather immigrated to the United States from Italy when he was 14 years old. He went to work as a florist at this very location and around the age of 40 was able to purchase the business. He became an American success story. He worked seven days a week, never took a vacation, and felt like the luckiest man on the planet. His sense of identity was rooted in his experience in World War I. He enlisted in the army and was awarded the Purple Heart for being wounded in action. These experiences gave his life a deep sense of meaning and purpose.

My dad and his brother eventually ran the family business. My two older brothers, my cousin, and I spent many hours at the shop after school and on holidays. On a daily basis we would experience a parade of lively characters sauntering in through the back door and regaling us with stories, jokes, and delightful snippets of information giving us a glimpse into the lives of many of the rich, wealthy, and ne'er-do-wells in the area.

My brothers, cousin, and I became quite adept at mimicking the exact quality and tone of each person's voice, people's mannerisms, as well as the way they walked into the room. My favorite was the head of parking for Brown University. His nickname was Lefty. He had this way of looking out of his left eye. He could see right through you. He would always stretch out my name and say to me, "*Raaahb!* I saw you walking around today with a new friend. She was a quite a looker, eh!"

Whenever our family got together for holiday dinners, it was inevitable that a stream of stories would emerge—some current and some timeless. The more they were told, the more embellished they would become. My grandfather would often recall the weekly occurrence, in the early years of the business, of one of the wealthier women in the area pulling up in front of the shop. Her driver would be wearing a chauffeur's hat, the rear door would swing open, and her leg would spill out onto the curb. Her piercing voice would come filtering into the shop . . . "Jaaames!" she would cry. My grandfather would jog out to the sidewalk to take care of her. He would always make the point that his job was to serve. And that's what he did best. My grandfather's dedication to his customers is what lingers with me most.

Stories are about family, culture, and connection. Stories celebrate our past, make sense of the present, and enable us to see a bright and hopeful future. Stories give us meaning and purpose.

In this chapter, we will look at the power of story as an essential tool of the transformational leader. We will look at what it means to step into the role of the leader of culture and to create meaning. We will distinguish the difference between story sharing and storytelling. In addition, we will explore what makes a great story, as well as what it takes to becoming a great storyteller.

THE POWER OF NARRATIVE

Marshall Ganz, a senior lecturer on public policy at Harvard's Kennedy School of Government, developed a framework called public narrative. It was born out of the civil rights movement of the 1960s where it was effectively used to inspire and mobilize large groups of people. He designed it as a way to articulate and translate our values into action.

Ganz posited that practicing leadership is about enabling others to achieve purpose in the face of uncertainty. It requires engaging the head, the heart, and the hands: strategy, motivation, and action. Through narrative we can articulate the experience of choice in the face of urgent challenge and we can learn how to draw on our values to manage the anxiety of agency, as well as exhilaration. We use narrative to engage the "head" and the "heart" as it both instructs and inspires—teaching us not only how we *ought* to act but motivating us *to act*—and thus engaging the "hands" as well.

Public narrative is woven from three elements of communication:

- **Story of Self**—communicates the values that are calling you to act. Your "why."

- **Story of Us**—communicates the values that are shared by those whom you hope to inspire to act.

- **Story of Now**—communicates the urgent challenge to those values that demands action now.

To understand motivation (that which inspires action), we must consider our emotions. Both share a root word, *motor*, which means "to move." Psychologists argue that information provided by our emotions, which we experience as feelings, is partly physiological, as when our respiration changes or our body temperature alters; partly behavioral, as when we are moved to advance, flee, or freeze; and partly cognitive, since we can describe what we feel as fear, love, desire, or joy.

But how then do we actually make decisions to act?

TIME TO ACT

Let me share with you how this book originated. It was May of 2017, and I was having coffee with Fred Green, chairman of the CEO Club of Boston. I was hoping that Fred would bring me in as a speaker at one of his meetings. Fred looked at me and said, "Rob, I really like your content and would like to bring you in as a speaker, but I can't." I asked him, "Why not?" Fred replied, "I only bring in people with books." To which I retorted, "Ha, sorry Fred, I don't have one!" He looked at me directly and said, "I know. The good news is that I know someone who helps people write them and get published. His name is Ken Lizotte, at Emerson Consulting Group. Send him an e-mail." Fred immediately gave me Ken's contact information. I sent a message to Ken, and we made a time to get together. At lunch we made a great connection and realized that we had a lot in common. We shared similar backgrounds, likes, and dislikes and had the same point of view in our work. He told me I definitely had a story to tell and that he knew he could get a publisher interested. He then laid out his proposal to me. This was a big undertaking, and I had no way of knowing if it would pan out. I asked him if he had any guarantees. He said no, but with confidence said that he only takes on people with whom he can be successful, and that he had an almost 100 percent success rate.

I told him to send me more information and that I would think about it.

But, how did I make my decision to act? Well, there were several things that enabled the decision to move forward with Ken. First, I did my research and gathered information from a variety of sources. I scoured the Internet and called several close friends who had written books and asked their opinions. In the end, I based my decision on how I felt about Ken. I instinctively felt that I could trust him. He was honest and forthcoming; he was someone that I knew I could work with, and that I felt had my best interests in mind. Along with that, I am a firm believer that when the bus pulls up and stops in front of your home and opens up its door, you hop on in. So, that is what I did.

WHAT DO EMOTIONS HAVE TO DO WITH ANYTHING?

Whenever you hear leaders say, "Emotions and feelings have no place in business," they are not being honest with you. Having a sense of meaning in our work has been shown to be a critical component to bringing our Best Self to our jobs. In the workplace, regardless of generation, every person wants three things: respect, meaningful and impactful work, and camaraderie. If you can be successful in speaking to what is important to others, what they value, and what gives them a sense of meaning and purpose, you will engage their emotions and stand a much better chance of gaining their trust and purposeful effort.

This is what it means to be a leader of culture.

LEADER OF CULTURE AND MEANING

If we think back at the Three Lenses model that was introduced in Chapter 6, we will remember that one of the perspectives of a leader is the cultural lens. This refers to the understanding of the underlying attitudes and beliefs held by the people who inhabit an organization. Why is this important? Because as humans we are essentially curious beings. We have a deep desire and need to create meaning from the environment and events that surround us. If we want to inspire and motivate others to purposeful action, we need to be able to speak to what moves people.

To be a leader of culture, we need to make a shift in our role and identity to that of chief meaning maker, cultural protagonist, and storyteller. In this role, we learn to develop and draw upon our narrative intelligence and story capabilities in order to become the advocate, champion, and standard bearer for the values and behaviors within the organization. It is our job to seek an understanding of the intrinsic motivations of the culture and begin to look at where people derive meaning in their work. In doing so, we go beyond our own myopic perspective and learn what it will take to enable change and encourage the adoption of new ideas.

THE ART OF STORYTELLING

We begin to develop our capacity to understand and lead culture by developing our narrative capability. We begin this process by mining for and extracting important moments in our personal and professional lives. Storytelling is the act of polishing and presenting these accounts in an intentional manner. Storytelling is the art of a leader. In his book *On Becoming a Leader*, Warren Bennis provides a clear path for developing our leadership potential. He says that the primary role of leaders is to look back upon their personal history and experiences, reflect upon the turning point moments of their lives, extract the values and lessons from these experiences, and share them in the form of stories.[1]

At the end of Chapter 7, you engaged in this process of story archeology. You identified your top three leadership values, as well as discovered a few gems or stories that best illustrate these values. The next step in the process is to polish these gems and begin to share them with others.

Having been an active storyteller for the past 40 years and teaching storytelling to business leaders for the past 20, I see the art of storytelling as having three distinct elements: the "why," the "how," and the "what."

The why of storytelling is about understanding the effective and strategic use of a story in a business context to convey complex information, to illustrate values, and to teach a lesson, as well as to break through a barrier and galvanize action.

Stories are:

- Attention grabbing

- Relatable and relevant

- Memorable and easily retold

The how of storytelling relates to knowing the structure of a good story, as well as having the confidence and ability to tell a great story. It's how to actually *be* a storyteller.

The what of storytelling is about choosing the right story for the right time that will achieve the results you are looking for. If you do this correctly, your story will speak to the "why" in the hearts of your audience.

Story Structure

There are many books and resources available that will explain to you the structure of a good story. You'll also learn what stories to tell in which situations. Why do we need this type of guidance? I think everyone has heard the "story" that leaders tell that goes, "times were hard, but we rallied, and now it's all good!" without any substance or specificity. Or alternatively, we have all heard leaders who focus on the wrong or uninteresting aspect of a story. These hollow frameworks don't make much impact. Knowing what makes up a great story is important.

Marshall Ganz provides an easy way to think about narrative structure. A story is made up of just three parts: the plot, the main character, and the moral or lesson the main character learns. Let's look at each.

- **The plot.** The plot is made up of three elements: a challenge, a choice, and an outcome. A story always begins by setting the scene. An actor is moving toward a desired goal, but then some kind of challenge appears. The plan is suddenly up in the air. The actor must figure out what to do. The person needs to make a choice and then live with the outcome.

- **The main character.** The main character, or the protagonist, is the person with whom we build an emotional connection. Main characters take us all the way inside of their struggle, their decision process, and the eventual outcome. They allow us to feel what they felt, and the story is relatable to our own lives.

- **The moral or lesson.** The reason we choose to use stories is to make a point, and to evoke a response. A good story, well told, will speak to our head by furnishing us with understanding, to our heart by giving us an emotional spark, and to our hands by providing us with a road map and the will to act.

BECOMING A STORYTELLER

The best storytellers make it look easy. As listeners we are immediately pulled in by the glint in their eyes, the cadence and variety in their voice, and the expression on their face. It's like they are telling the story with their whole body. We are particularly captured by how they make us feel.

Great storytellers are willing to open themselves up and allow us to be in the story with them. We feel what they feel. We see what they see. And, most of all, we gain the realization and insight from the experience that they have had. Their story is our story.

Have you ever led a large project or initiative where you felt the energy begin to drain and the momentum begin to wane when it was about 80 percent complete? I would imagine you have at one time or another.

What did you do? How did you reengage your team toward the finish line?

While teaching a program in Canada a few years back, I asked these exact questions to the group. I then asked if any of them had ever had a similar experience in another part of their lives.

One fellow, John, raised his hand and explained,

> I am a runner. I run marathons and last year I ran the Boston Marathon. It was a hot day and this took a toll on many of the runners. As I hit Heartbreak Hill I was exhausted. Everything hurt, every muscle screamed, the hard pavement reverberated painfully through my feet and my legs, and I just wanted to sit down. As I lost momentum, I found myself thinking, "It's ok . . . you've done enough . . . just sit down . . . no one will care . . . you did enough . . . it will be ok . . ."
>
> I slowed to a complete stop. I bent over and put my hands on my knees for balance. In this moment I began to visualize my wife and daughters eagerly waiting for me at the finish line. They invested so much in my training. I could not have gotten this far without them. I imagined myself going into work and having everyone ask me about the race, over and over, and the shame I would feel when I told them I did not finish.

Suddenly, a deep feeling of pride and resolve came over me. I felt a rush of adrenaline surge through my body and I sprang into action. I had the strongest finish ever.

I learned something about myself that day. That I have resources within me I never knew that I had, and that those resources are inextricably tied to what is most important to me. Respect, appreciation, and love for my friends, family, and self. I know deep in my heart that I could never and would never let them down.

The room was glued to John as he told this story. Every eye was on him. Every ear was open. Everyone in the room got the message and loudly applauded. Why?

When John told us about his experience at the Boston Marathon, he spoke naturally. He did not think about the structure of the story, he just told it. He was fully immersed inside of the experience. When he did this, he brought us inside the story with him, captured our imaginations, and triggered our emotions.

He naturally exhibited a sense of poise and presence. He naturally showed vulnerability when he described his inner struggle. He revealed his strength of character, resolve, and resilience. We experienced him as being authentic. The interesting thing is that he told his story at the beginning of the session before we had even started teaching the skills of storytelling.

The question in theater is always "Can you repeat it?" Could John capture the same natural quality, flow, and presence if he told it to us again? This question is why skill development is so important.

As the story goes, the legendary British actor Sir Laurence Olivier stepped off of the stage after a particularly brilliant performance cursing under his breath and wearing a scowl. As his assistant began helping him take off his cloak he asked, "You just gave one of the most remarkable performances ever. Why are you so angry?"

To which Olivier replied, "Yes, it was brilliant. I . . . I just don't know what I did!"

So many ask, "How do we repeat our brilliant results?" But this is the wrong question. The answer to "How can we repeat the approach that got results?" is much more important. There is a difference between consistency of method and consistency of effect. As a leader, do you focus only on driving results? Or do you focus on your approach and intent? Intention gives rise to technique, "how" you are going to get the results. This is what it takes to be a great storyteller and is what it takes to be a great leader.

Theater Approach to Storytelling

A good story cannot be devised; it has to be distilled.
—RAYMOND CHANDLER

By now I hope that you've bought into the idea that stories are a useful tool in business. You have become familiar with the structure of a good story, as well as what types of stories work in various situations. But, have you ever actually summoned up the courage to tell a story? Do you wonder how to employ a story in a presentation or client sales meeting? Do you feel confident in your ability to tell a great one?

I was fortunate to have studied the art of storytelling as a central part of my theater training and performances. I was taught to engage with my audience members after each performance—to ask them what they liked or did not like. In one instance, a dad mentioned to me that he "felt transported" by my story. This was a revelation. When you immerse yourself completely in both the rehearsal and performance process, something magical happens to your audience. Your audience naturally becomes immersed in the story with you . . . and they are transported.

Direct Narrative Storytelling

Direct narrative storytelling is the process of engulfing the listener in a story full of texture and details and transports the audience to another time and place. Whether telling your own story, a folktale, or someone else's story, the storyteller will take on the persona of the main character and bring the story to life through his or her own eyes.

Most direct narrative stories are told in the first person, present tense, such as, "I am standing at the edge of a high cliff. I feel a tinge of excitement as I grasp the handrail and look into the canyon." One can also tell a direct narrative in the third person, such as, "He steps outside of the building only to be blown back by the immense wind." Both are full of rich details, emotions, and action.

The medium makes a difference as to whether telling a story in the present or past tense might be best. Will people be listening to you or reading your story? If you look back throughout this book, you will notice that most stories I have shared are told in the past tense and a few in the present tense. If someone is writing an open letter to an organization, for example, past tense can often be the more "readable" elegant tense for conveying meaning. However, if you are about to step onto a stage and engage your team and want to truly involve them in your story, the present tense is the most effective approach.

First person storytelling takes some practice, but utilizing the first person and present tense allows you to reexperience the event. It allows you to enter into the experience and bring it to life. It also allows you to express through your face, body, and voice the emotions that you were experiencing at that time. Can you see where the physical and vocal theater exercises that we practiced in Chapter 4 come in handy? When we have developed a larger range of both physical and vocal expression we are better able to bring our stories to life.

Engage Your Audience with Sensory Details

As you step into your story, it is critical to bring the details of your experience to life. By this, I mean the details that we experience through our senses. These include, what we see, hear, feel, smell, and taste. The background sounds of the environment, fragrances, aromas, and smells either draw us in or repel us. The relaxation we feel from the heat in Florida, as well the shiver we feel from the fear of walking down a dark alley, both make us feel something.

When combined, these elements of direct narrative storytelling make our stories irresistible for audiences. They can actually smell the popcorn emanating from the break room, they can feel the delight you experienced when you crossed the finish line, and they internalize the lessons you learned when you were knocked down, only to get back up and complete your long-awaited goal. These are the qualities of storytelling that allow others to experience for themselves where you are, who you are, and what you are feeling and thinking.

Now that you understand the power of sensory details to grab an audience's attention, the next step in the process is editing the details to only those that forward the action of the story. If you remember my story in Chapter 8, "I was sitting at my desk finishing up an e-mail to a client. It was the end of a long and hard week, but a good one. I could smell the popcorn from down the hall and hear the laughter of my colleagues gathering in the break room. I knew there was a cold beer waiting for me." These elements served to engage you visually as well as make you aware of your emotional need for connection and relief at the end of a long week.

Art and Science

In late 2017, I partnered with Debbi Bromley, the senior vice president of HR for Genex Services, LLC, a managed care provider in workers' compensation. She had been getting her EdD with a specialty in innovation and leadership. The focus of her dissertation was on the effectiveness of theater techniques to influence a leader's self-efficacy and performance in storytelling. Self-efficacy refers to the belief in one's ability. Performance refers to the actual doing of the activity. The findings of the study incorporated both quantitative and qualitative data.

We utilized my two-day program as the foundation for her study. At the beginning of the program we recorded each person delivering a prepared three-minute presentation that incorporated a story. I was fascinated by their diverse interpretations of what a story was and how to use a story in a business presentation. To some, it was just a list of facts. To others, they would make a point that it was "quite a story," but never really told it. To others, the idea of a story was not evident at all in their presentations. And a few of them seemed to really know what they were doing. Their stories came alive. These were the presentations that had an immediate impact on us.

What Did We Do?

During the two days, the participants were introduced to a variety of theater exercises designed to build the poise and presence of a storyteller. This first involved entering, landing, and filling a space with an energized and alert presence. We used Shakespearean text to bring words alive, clarify our intention, and engage and connect with audience members. We took the time to share Best Self stories. We also practiced the use of metaphoric images filled with sensory details as a means of communicating complex information clearly and concisely.

The final exercise focused on teaching the skills of first person, or *direct narrative storytelling*. We split the participants into pairs with one playing the role of the storyteller and the other as the coach. Each storyteller was asked to choose one story and then led through a series of five rounds of developmental coaching. Each round consisted of the storyteller sharing and the coach providing specific and direct feedback.

- The first round encouraged the storyteller to use first person, present tense, and sensory details.

- The second round concentrated on enhancing the vocal elements of the story by incorporating environmental sounds, character voices, and reflecting the emotional intensity of the story.

- In the third round, storytellers were asked to tell their stories without any words and to focus strictly on the gestures, physicality, and actions of the characters. This was perplexing to the storytellers at first but ultimately created a room full of leaping, crouching, and tiptoeing storytellers.

- The fourth round gave the storytellers an opportunity to put all of these elements together into a cohesive whole.

- The last and most important round gave the coach and storyteller an opportunity to check the structure of the story to ensure that the context was set, a main character was present, and it was focused on a goal, introduced a challenge, had a choice point, and landed us at an outcome. The pair then discussed and extracted a lesson from the experience as well as a potential application for the story.

- Each person then had the opportunity to share his or her story in front of the group and receive additional feedback and coaching.

What Did We Learn?

In the last section of the program, we took the time for each person to prepare, rehearse, and deliver his or her initial presentation again. The participants were encouraged to incorporate all of the techniques learned over the two days into their stories. The results were remarkable.

- Each and every person was better able to step into the circle and engage with us, their audience.

- They seemed to relish and embrace their role as a storyteller.

- They were able to deploy a solid structure for their presentation that included a plot, main character, and lesson.

- They were able to bring their stories to life in the direct narrative form.

After the sessions, Debbi gathered both qualitative and quantitative data from the participants. From the survey data several key themes emerged indicating enhanced self-efficacy and performance capabilities. These themes are represented in Figure 9.1.

In addition, the themes shown in Figure 9.2 emerged regarding the perception of change gathered from the individuals who viewed both the pre- and post-performances recorded in the program. The watchers were given specific criteria on which to view the recordings. Their perceptions mirror those experienced by a real audience.

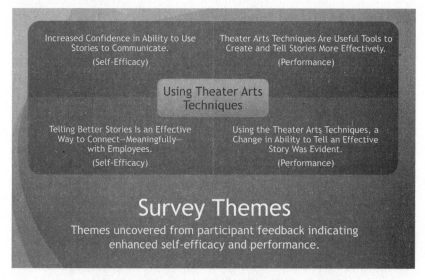

Survey Themes

Themes uncovered from participant feedback indicating enhanced self-efficacy and performance.

FIGURE 9.1 **Themes discovered by survey participants indicating enhanced self-efficacy and performance**

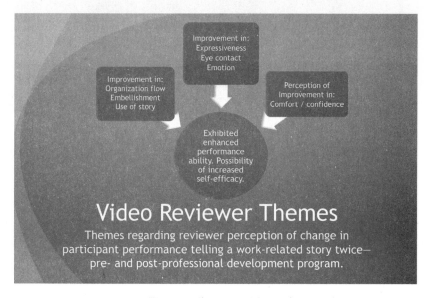

Video Reviewer Themes

Themes regarding reviewer perception of change in participant performance telling a work-related story twice— pre- and post-professional development program.

FIGURE 9.2 **Themes discovered from video review of pre- and post-performance**

And finally, the slide presented in Figure 9.3 was derived from follow-up feedback from participants suggesting that the theater arts techniques learned in the program resulted in the participant's perception of an increase in his or her ability (performance) and confidence (self-efficacy) to tell a great story.

As one of the participants reported:

> Dear classmates, today I gave my speech and used the storytelling model Rob taught us. Out of my normal comfort zone but it worked! Thanks for all of your help and encouragement.

Confidence is built through trial and error. One must feel that the reward far outweighs the risk of embarrassment and failure. It also helps us when we see someone else take a step forward and succeed. Storytelling is a human artform. It is in the process of telling and receiving that we build deep connection and understanding.

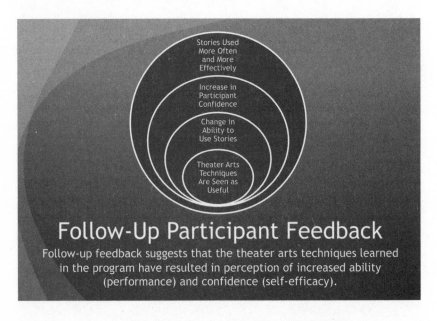

FIGURE 9.3 **Follow-up feedback from participants**

Stepping into the Fire—What Would You Do?

Anytime change happens in an organization, there is a high level of uncertainty and fear. This is when it is most important to be transparent, show a bit of vulnerability, and let people know what they can expect from you.

Picture this: You have just been promoted from leading a team of 25 people to leading a team of 250. For the past five years you have been the head of one of the most innovative parts of the organization. Everyone on your former team understood who you were, what you stood for, and what they could expect from you. You were fair, firm, and formidable. They believed in you and trusted you.

Now, you have been chosen to step into a new and highly visible role tasked with consolidating five separate teams into one. A few people know you, but most have never met you or even heard about you. The stakes are high and the organization is depending upon you to deliver results. A town hall meeting has been planned, and you are the main attraction. This will be your introduction to your entire team.

If you're going to step in front of a large team with a difficult message, how do you prepare? What do you say? Do you move right into action, or do you take a moment to make an authentic connection? Take a look at the fictionalized story below as an example of how this might play out.

Thank you all for coming today. I understand how difficult it must be for all of you right now. It was only 10 years ago when I sat in your very same seat. The company that I was working for was going through a merger, and we were awash in a sea of uncertainty. I had a small family at the time and did not know if I was going to have a job the next day. It was a terrifying moment.

Today is a different day. Most of you don't know who I am and what you can expect. To be honest with you, I cannot give you any answers today regarding the impact of the recent restructuring. What I can give you is a promise. To give each and every one of you a voice and to treat you fairly.

You might be thinking, "Sure, it's easy to say that, but how can we be sure that you will keep your promise?"

Let me tell you a story.

It is October in my senior year of high school, and I'm a third-string quarterback on the football team. I'm the backup to the backup. Just after lunch, I'm at my locker getting my books for my next class. The hallway is packed with kids filing back and forth. I hear the sounds of locker doors slamming shut, and the lingering aroma of french fries fills the air.

Suddenly, there is a commotion coming from down the hall. I see a group of the starting football players gathered in a circle laughing and pointing. They are towering over and taunting someone who is lying on the floor. It is Steven, the new kid in our class. He has cerebral palsy. His books are in a pile next to him. All of his papers are strewn across the floor, and he is crying.

I walk over to take a closer look and stop in my tracks. I think to myself, "This is wrong." But what could I do about it? These are the stars of the team. Suddenly I feel a wave of anger and find myself stepping into the middle of the circle.

I stand tall. I look them all in the eye and, in a voice I didn't know I had, forcefully tell them to back off. I pick up the papers and books off of the floor and help Steven to his feet. I make sure to put his crutches back on his forearms. I put my arm around him and help him get to his next class.

I never said a word to the players who stood around and taunted Steven. However, each of them came to me and personally apologized. They also promised to personally apologize to Steven. It was a lesson in tolerance and respect I don't think any of them will forget. To this day, Steven is one of my best friends.

The reason I tell you this story is because sometimes it's important to stand up for what's right, even when it's not easy or popular. As I said, I cannot give you any answers today, but I can promise to be fully transparent with you all in our decision-making process. If you see or experience something that does not feel right, speak up. Each member of my team is onboard and ready to address your concern and answer any questions that you might have. My door is always open to you.

The connection that the speaker would want from his audience is "I will do what's right, even if it isn't easy." Sure, he could have just said these words to his new team, but how do you think they would have responded? By telling a story about himself, it revealed his true character and the audience walked away with a memorable experience of this leader's authenticity.

Make Your Story Land with Your Audience

Choosing the right story for the right moment is critical. We want to make sure that we are sharing a story that will resonate with the audience that we are addressing. As we did in this last story, we need to think about the questions and concerns that are in the minds of the audience. What do they need to hear from us that will resonate authentically and put them at ease? This will give us a clue as to the right type of story to tell, as well as the elements that we need to reveal in the story.

Once you have identified your top three leadership values, begin to search for moments and experiences that best illustrate and bring that value to life. Sometimes it could just be an inspirational quote or analogy. No matter what they are, they are tools to carry with you at all times. It is important not to overplay them, but tell them enough to different audiences so that they stay fresh and become richer over time.

When using stories in a business presentation, it is important to identify specific stories that match up with your key points. Take a look at the flipchart shown in Figure 9.4. This came from a recent presentation I did around building high-performing teams. I have three key points on the page:

- Personal Commitment to Growth
- Expand Beyond Your Comfort Zone of Relating
- Build the Relational Fabric of Your Team Through Story Sharing

If you look closely, you will see small words on the left side of the chart. These refer to the stories that I will tell to describe each of the points. Let me give you an example of a story that I used to illustrate the last bullet on the chart, "Building the Relational Fabric of Your Team Through Story Sharing."

In a recent program I had two senior women leaders from a global financial services firm. On the second day of the session, they both were excited and eager to share their experience from the prior evening. One said, "We have been working on the same team for 10 years. Our offices sit right next to each other. Six weeks ago, our leader had asked us to work on a budget proposal together. Until last night, we had not made time for each other. After doing this exercise together, we decided to go out for a bite to eat. The stories continued to pour out. While at dinner, we decided to work on the

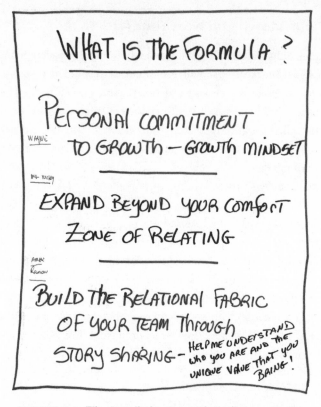

FIGURE 9.4 Flipchart listing key points of presentation

budget proposal. It took us a total of 10 minutes to get it done! We sent it off to our boss who was thrilled by the quality of the work. In about an hour, I knew more about my partner than I had in the 10 years of working together. And look at the results we were able to achieve in such a short amount of time. I now get the importance of relationship building in business.

The story was clear, succinct, and resonated with my audience.

How to choose what stories to tell and what elements to draw out of your audience is the true art of storytelling. You must read the audience and, in the moment, determine how long or quickly you will tell it. The best rule of thumb is to try each story out with a friend or colleague to determine if it will hit the mark. Ask for feedback to see if you need to polish it more or highlight one particular part more than another.

ONE CAVEAT

There is one thing I want to be sure to clarify. There is a difference between sharing something that is personal and something that is private. A personal story is one that holds meaning and significance to you. It is something with which you hold no shame. A private story could be one that is still a bit too raw and one that you don't fully understand yet. What you choose to share and not to share is a personal choice. This also comes with experience. If you are ever unsure, ask someone that you trust before sharing it with a wider audience.

THE CHAPTER IS OVER BUT
THE STORY CONTINUES

We covered a lot of ground in this chapter. We discussed what it means for a leader to step into the role of the chief meaning maker and cultural protagonist. We discussed the "why," "how," and "what" of stories, as well as a variety of story structures. And finally, we went into depth on what it takes to become a great storyteller. The next step is to begin gathering, developing, and sharing the stories that truly matter to you and to those that you serve.

THE ART OF
INFLUENCING

To be persuasive we must be believable; to be believable
we must be credible; to be credible we must be truthful.
Influence is the central competence, the ultimate ability
of a person to alter or persuade the thoughts,
beliefs and actions of an individual or a group.
—EDWARD R. MURROW

nderstanding the sources of influence and power within organizations is crucial when leading from your Best Self. Throughout this chapter we will focus on the development of personal power as the most sustainable way for leaders to create meaningful action. We will also explore key communication tools, including the power of metaphor, to open others to your ideas and guide action. We will also learn how to use the power of intention to galvanize your expressive capabilities and maximize the impact of your messages. Before diving into each topic, it's important to understand that the ultimate responsibility of executives and leaders is to influence, and by that I mean:

- To influence themselves and how they choose to show up and lead
- To influence the language of their organization
- To influence the vision and strategy of their organization
- To influence potential customers to trust them and purchase their services

- To influence their teams to take on a collective goal with purpose, passion, and relentless effort

So where does influence come from? What does it look like? Is it the same as power? How can you develop it? What are the tools of influence?

Influence can be defined as:

- The ability to impact an individual's beliefs and actions
- The act of producing an effect without the use of force

Power can be defined as:

- The capacity to directly affect behavior and affect outcomes

Simply put, power is the ability to influence someone else. Influencing requires power.

WHERE DOES POWER COME FROM?

A study conducted by John French and Bertrand Raven in 1959 still stands as the benchmark for sources of power that leaders use to influence others. French and Raven identified five sources of power that can be grouped into two categories: organizational power (legitimate, reward, and coercive) and personal power (expert and referent).

Let's take a look at French and Raven's five sources of power. The first three are "organizational powers" (referring to one's position in an organization), and the following two are "personal powers" (referring to one's individual capabilities).

Organizational Power

- *Legitimate (positional) power* is a person's ability to influence others' behavior because of the position that person holds within the organization. Those with legitimate or positional power have the understood right to ask others to do things that are considered within their scope of authority. At the most simplistic level, a manager could, on the basis of her position in the organization, conceivably ask any subordinate in her office to sharpen the pencils on their desk. It might seem silly, but I've seen it done.

- *Reward power* is a person's ability to influence others' behavior by providing them with the things they want to receive. Rewards are usually grouped into three types: financial (a bonus or raise), work-related (a desired assignment or project), and recognition (and award, acknowledgment, etc.). A manager's behavior can change if there are appropriate reward systems in place for specific behaviors. But the power only works if the person receiving the rewards values them.

- *Coercive power* is a person's ability to influence others' behavior by the use of punishment or threat. Typical organizational punishments include reprimands, undesirable work assignments, withholding key information, demotion, suspension, or dismissal. Coercive power has negative side effects, resulting in negative feelings toward those who use it.

Personal Power

- *Expert (knowledge) power* is a person's ability to influence others' behavior because of recognized knowledge, skills, or abilities. Experts have power even when they rank low in the organization's hierarchy. To be granted expert power, others must perceive the power holder to be credible, trustworthy, and relevant.

- *Reverent power* is a person's ability to influence others' behavior by gaining their respect and admiration. Reverent power develops out of the words, deeds, and reputation of an individual.

Leaders who exercise organizational power can surely get a certain amount of attention and compliance from those that they lead. However, reliance on any of these types of power is limited in scope and long-term impact. People get tired and resentful of the carrot or stick approach to leading.

On the other side of the equation, leaders who embody either aspect of personal power have the ability to engender trust in others. It explains why some people will "walk through walls" for their leaders. These are the leaders who inspire loyalty and trust and can ignite an entire organization around a common purpose.

A FRAMEWORK FOR INFLUENCE

Let's consider the following as a model for developing personal power and influence. It has three main areas of focus:

- *Poise and presence* to create impact

- *Empathy* to create trust and connection

- *Language* to create meaning

Poise and Presence

In the opening chapters of this book we worked on the skills of poise and presence. We learned that our presence has a clear and direct impact on how others experience us and how they experience themselves when they are with us. We learned that others are either drawn to or diverted from the energy that we project. We learned that our physical and vocal presence can send conflicting messages without our awareness, and that we need to develop the skill and mastery of our body language and vocal flexibility in order to support the messages that we want to communicate.

We also focused on developing the inner dimensions of presence and authenticity. It is only when we truly know what we stand for and can embody these values and principles in our daily behaviors and interactions that others will, in turn, be open to our ideas and invest themselves into a collective future.

Empathy

Empathy is the development of relational intelligence. We learned that authentic connection relies upon the unquestionable quality of our presence, our listening skills, and our respect of another person's values, beliefs, and differences—in the moment, eyeball to eyeball.

When these conditions exist, others feel safe enough to bring their Best Self forward. When we create these conditions, we experience a reciprocal feeling of connectedness.

Language

Language is the development of narrative intelligence. We learned the power of story to engage the head, heart, and hands in Chapter 9. As leaders, it is critical for us to become great communicators.

KEYS TO GREAT COMMUNICATION

Let's explore some of the tools and techniques that you can use to influence others in your day-to-day communication.

Opening up Others to Our Ideas

Have you ever made a presentation and felt as though you were speaking to a wax museum? I can imagine you chuckling and nodding your head. Well, I hate to break it to you, but that's not the audience's fault.

When an audience listens to a presentation, they utilize the analytical parts of their brains. It's as though they are in a comedy club waiting for the first comic to appear and make them laugh. It's your job to move them away from analysis and shift to the visual and emotional parts of their brains.

For a moment, and without closing your eyes, picture the home that you grew up in. Picture yourself standing on the front lawn or sidewalk. Can you see the color of your home? The trees around it? The windows and doors? You just accessed the visual part of your brain. It's that easy!

However, it is not enough just to create great imagery. We need to appeal to both the visual and emotional parts of a person's brain. The image needs to both be vivid and hold significance to the person. Metaphors and stories open up others to your ideas by creating these vivid images in their minds and emotional connections in their hearts.

Indirect Narrative

Humans are meaning-making beings. If you create a line drawing, people will fill in the colors. This is an example of an indirect narrative.

Indirect narrative is when you cast the audience as the main character or protagonist of the story. You give them the opportunity to fill in the picture with their own experiences and create personal meaning. This style of storytelling is best employed when you want to bring your vision to life. You literally put your audience into a particular moment. Provide them with visual imagery and other sensory details that are a part of your plan. Let them feel, see, hear, and smell the environment. They will let you know if they like it and what it means to them.

By activating people's senses, you can also combat confirmation bias. Confirmation bias is when we use information and data to confirm a previously held opinion or belief. For example, I have worked with people who have said that someone in their new company looks just like their last boss, whom they did not like very much at all. Somehow, they formed a negative opinion about this new person based on their prior experience. This is not rational, but it happens. Why is this important? Confirmation bias is a potent force. It takes skill to overcome it.

The point here is that you cannot deal with it directly.

Think of times when you have tried to convince someone of something. The energy of convincing tends to create a defensive response. It's not unlike when you walk into a car dealership and a young salesperson greets you with a larger-than-life smile and immediately starts pushing. Whereas seasoned salespeople take their time. They can read your body language and know that your defenses are up. Their job is to get you to sit in the car and give you a sensory experience. The experience itself will begin to influence how you feel. And they know that no matter how much research a customer has done, people buy a car based on how they feel about it.

We're not selling cars, but we are trying to move people in a particular direction. One of the most powerful ways to do this is through immersing our audience in visual and emotional imagery. We can capture their focus and attention and influence how they see, think, and feel about a person, idea, or situation.

The Power of Metaphor

Aristotle once said, "The greatest thing by far is to be a master of metaphor." Figures of speech such as metaphor or simile and extended analogy are the most powerful communication tools for the leader. The very way we think and reason is metaphoric, so the use of metaphors goes to the roots of the way we process information and make decisions. That's why fixing an idea in a good metaphor carries such power.

Metaphors are all around us. They are a part of the fabric of our language. Every culture has them. Phrases such as "time is money," "smart as a fox," and "a force of nature" are English-based idioms that are used on a daily basis and in every part of our lives. However, using metaphors in a conscious and strategic manner is a learned skill and does not come as easily to some as it does to others.

One of my favorite stories of the use of a strategic metaphor comes from a former client, Mike, the VP of marketing at a large pharmaceutical company.

Mike told me about a time he had to present to his entire marketing team of 200. As he walked out onto the stage he carried with him a four-foot stick. He paused and greeted his audience, and with a smile he asked, "I guess you are wondering why I am carrying this stick?

"The length of this stick is exactly four feet, eight and a half inches. This is the exact distance between the rails of a railroad track. It is also the exact distance between the ruts created by the chariot wheels in the city of Pompeii. This distance was determined by the width of two horses pulling a vehicle and was kept constant so the wheels of the wagons could ride in the ruts and not get broken.

"This distance has not changed in centuries. Now I know that we have been going through a lot of change these days and that it has caused some concern among you. What I want you to remember are the things that remain constant throughout this process, and those are our values and how we treat each other. As long as these remain constant, we will stay intact."

Mike was a master of metaphor. Key learnings:

- **Metaphors are magnetic.** He was able to focus the attention of the room quickly.

- **Metaphors are meaningful.** Everyone in the room got the message. It landed with them.

- **Metaphors are memorable.** It's been over a decade since I first heard this metaphor, and it remains vivid in my mind.

Select Your Metaphor Carefully

In a recent conversation with one of my coaching clients at MIT, I was amazed at how skillfully she applied an analogy to build engagement around a new AGILE approach to a cloud computing project. The issue she addressed was based on the group's initial evaluation of risk. People were voicing skepticism when problems began to surface in the project causing delays. She quickly gathered the group together to address their concerns. She said to the group, "I understand that you are worried about the current problems with the project. If you remember our initial presentation, we identified that we are entering into new territory and that there would be a certain level of risk. However, by adopting the AGILE approach, we would be better able to meet and overcome these challenges. Think about it like this: We are in the process of building a new home. Our home. As anyone who has ever built and then moved into a new home understands, there are unforeseen issues that inevitably crop up. The point is this: When it is your home, you are much better prepared to deal with these issues. Our commitment to this project is no different. We are here to stay, and we are well equipped to deal with whatever comes our way."

Her analogy was well received and began to spread around the work environment. One of her colleagues became a bit competitive and tried to employ an analogy of his own. In a subsequent presentation to the same group he used the analogy of the group being on an airplane and having to do updates and changes while in flight. The group, knowing the original analogy, pushed back. They voiced dissatisfaction with his image, saying they were not interested in joining him on a broken airplane. It would be too dangerous. They would much prefer to be in their own home where they had the opportunity to work things out in a safe manner. He eventually saw his error and fully embraced the image that my client offered to her team.

I was impressed at the power that my client's analogy had on her work group, and even more astonished at the visceral reaction the group had to the unsuccessful image used by her colleague.

Don't underestimate the power that a well-crafted analogy has on those that you lead.

As with any new skill or capability, we need to understand:

- Its intrinsic value

- Why it would be important for us to learn

- How to develop the discipline to make it a natural part of our communication repertoire

The key is to put it into practice right away.

So, how could you use a metaphor in your role as a leader? Let's brainstorm:

- *You organized a conference and will be introducing all of the speakers for the day. Do you wait for them to give you their bio and then read it awkwardly to the audience?*

     You might, but you shouldn't. Instead, take a few minutes to have a short conversation with each presenter. Ask them to tell you something surprising or unique about themselves. What impressions do you have of each person? How do they make you feel? What is remarkable about them? Can you come up with a meaningful image that the audience would appreciate? Condense it and present it. Make each introduction a little different, but equally personal, connected, and inspiring. By the end of the day you will be a master of introductions.

- *You are a manager of a team and are excited about your new hire. She brings the unique perspective, critical capability, and experience you have been looking for. You want to inspire the current members to reach out and get to know this new person. How can you frame the introduction so that they will be more likely to do so?*

  Take the time to have an in-depth conversation with your new hire. Share stories. Discover what makes them interesting as a person and uniquely qualified for the role. Search for an image or metaphor that describes the value that the person brings to the team. Use the image to bring your message to life.

- *You are a partner in a start-up company, and you and your partner are about to make a pitch to a venture group. Unfortunately, your partner is sick and unable to join you. You show up, engage the group, and make your presentation. Immediately after you finish, one of them says, "We love your idea, we think you are fantastic, and also know that your partner was not able to make it today. What makes her special? What do you value about her?" What do you say that will positively influence the way they see your partner?*

  This is where an image or metaphor can be powerful. Use the template below to guide your preparation process.

  - Let me tell you about _____

  - What I appreciate about him/her is

  _____

  - He/she possesses three key attributes that make him/her a dream partner:

    1. _____
    2. _____
    3. _____

  - I think of him/her like

  _____

  _____

Find an image or metaphor that would capture their imagination. Use visual and sensory details to grab their attention and create a meaningful connection.

. . .

Becoming a master of metaphor takes commitment and practice. The beauty is that the more you practice, the better you'll get at it. The images just start to come.

THE POWER OF INTENTION

If you remember back to Chapters 3 and 4, we learned that expanding our physical presence and being aware of our facial gestures can have a large impact on how others experience us and receive our messages. We used Shakespearean text to help us enhance the flexibility and range of our voices. We do this in order to better convey emotional qualities that convey meaning to others.

In communication, our intention amplifies our gestures, voice, and emotion in a way that will have the most impact on our intended audience. This is the primary mechanism that actors use to interpret the words that they will say, in order to achieve their desired outcome.

Let's put this in action and use some more words from Shakespeare's play *Julius Caesar*.

Friends, Romans, countrymen, lend me your ears!

As you might recall, Caesar was the first emperor of Rome. He was brutally murdered by a small group of Roman senators in the Forum. As with anything that happens behind closed doors, the message spreads fast. The senators needed to get ahead of things and try to control the message.

Caesar's body was laid out on the steps in front of the Forum to a very large assembly of people, all looking for guidance on what to think and feel about the events that had just transpired. The first to speak was Brutus. He was like a son to Caesar (as well as the chief conspirator in his murder). Brutus was also a trained orator. He understood the Greek model of communication: logos, ethos, and pathos.

- *Logos* is an appeal to logic. Someone utilizing logos persuades others through reason and facts.

- *Ethos* is an appeal to ethics and values, or uses the character and credibility of the person to influence.

- *Pathos* is an appeal to the emotions and heart of one's audience to draw others over to your side. In other words, this is the emotional effect of your words.

Brutus created a powerful speech primarily through the use of logos and ethos. He said all the right things and stood tall as a Roman senator. However, his speech was devoid of emotion and connection. It left his audience searching for meaning.

Then it was Marc Antony's turn. He was Caesar's general. He loved Caesar and was not about to be blamed for his murder. He needed to make a strong and emotional appeal to this crowd. His life depended upon it.

He begins with the words *"Friends, Romans, countrymen, lend me your ears!"*

Let's think about the intention behind each of these words. If you like, you can visit my website for a short video where I walk you through this exercise (www.leadingfromyourbestself.com/ch10-influencing).

- **Friends.** He needs to feel like he has at least one friend in the crowd. He looks directly at his closest ally with the intention *to connect* with that person. He holds his hands out and says the word, "Friends."

- **Romans.** He sees the closest members of his regiment. The men with whom he has fought side by side. They need him to be strong for them and acknowledge and affiliate with them. He gathers all of his energy with the intent *to rouse* and bellows, "Romans." Can you bring this to life? This one is fun especially if you use the vocal and physical presence of your audience to get them to repeat it back to you.

- **Countrymen.** He needs to appeal to everyone in the crowd. To bring them together and make them feel a part. He needs *to inspire* them. This is where you can use your wide arms when you shout the word, "Countrymen."

- **Lend me your ears.** Then he needs to ask them to listen. This is where you can be a bit creative to see how intention can transform your communication.

Try shifting intentions, *to plead*, for instance. How does that intention change the delivery? What does it do to the sound of your voice and the gesture that you use? Intentionality creates congruence in our communication. Our voice, body, and emotions are all communicating the same message. People experience us as authentic and believable. Try some other intentions, such as *to invite*, or *to command*.

Below is a list of various intentions that you can use to guide what you say, how you say it, and ultimately how people respond to you.

- To shake up

- To reassure

- To warn

- To inspire

- To admonish

- To praise

- To energize

- To enlighten

Using Intention in a Business Situation

On a recent call, one of my coaching clients asked for my help with a presentation for her entire sales team. She was terrified to speak in front of these 30 people in just a few days. I asked her to describe the situation. She said that her company was laying off 15 percent of the workforce and she was worried about how to speak to her team about it. I asked if any of the folks on her team were being laid off. No, she said, adding, "We need them now more than ever!" I then asked her what she thought her team was thinking and feeling. She paused and said, "scared, nervous, angry," "Am I being laid off?," "How will this impact my ability to work?," and "Will I continue to be able to support my family?"

I supported her thoughts and then asked her what they needed from her. She was quick and said, "to reassure." She was exactly right.

Take a moment and put yourself in the shoes of this person. Write down some words that you might say as you step in front of your team of 30 members in the midst of company layoffs. How could you incorporate some of the elements that we have introduced so far in this chapter and book? Would you step right in and start talking? Or would you step in front of them, take a moment, and breathe? Let the moment sink in. Smile, look at one person, take another breath, and land with that person.

The second option allows you to open yourself up to the group before you start to speak. Can you allow the intention "to reassure" to guide how you say the words that you wrote down?

Begin to think through the entire scenario. Is that all you are going to say? What else do you need from them? You may need "to challenge" them to dig deep and find meaning and purpose in their work, because it is their effort that is going to lift the organization out of its current troubles. And finally, you could "instill confidence" in them and let them know that you will be with them every step of the way.

This is a powerful way to craft meaningful messages. It is the combination of empathy and intention that allows you to meet people where they are and move them to where they did not know they wanted to go. One builds true executive presence—through embracing leadership moments, stepping into the fire, and truly leading others.

PAUSE POINT

No matter how well you can work a room or craft an inspiring memo, people are smart; they can see right through a disingenuous message. Sincerity and authenticity cannot be scripted. The truth eventually wins out. However, there are still countless leaders who lead with lies and deception. As Groucho Marx once quacked, "Sincerity is the key to success. Once you can fake that, you've got it made."

Trust is built from the ground up. Once you make a promise, be sure to follow through on it. Once trust is lost, it is very difficult to regain.

PREPARATION

How you prepare for any interaction or presentation needs to be a critical part of your communication process. Have you thought about who will be sitting in the audience? Have you reflected on what these people might be thinking and feeling? What might be their fears and concerns? What do you need from you right now?

Empathy can be a difficult concept to understand and put into practice. One of the ways to exercise empathy is to reflect upon the words that people might be thinking and feeling. In this case, they might be thinking things like:

- Can I trust you?
- What will happen to us?
- Will I still have my job or be made "redundant"?
- How will I take care of my family if I lose this job?

I think you get where I am going. Many leaders are ill prepared for these "leadership moments." Doing some thoughtful self-reflection is the first step to hitting your mark in these types of situations. Reach out to your trusted advisors to unearth some of the themes and stories from the group. Reflect on your own experience for times when you might have been in the same position as they are now.

Presentation Preparation Worksheet

In advance of any situation or presentation, it's important to do an appropriate amount of preparation. Thinking about the specifics of the situation and considering the point of view of all key stakeholders is critical to landing your message. Choose an upcoming situation where you must present and address a critical issue, and use the questions listed here as a template.

Who is your audience? What is the situation?

_____

_____

_____

What is your overall goal for your presentation?

_____

_____

_____

What is the headline message that you need to communicate?

_____

_____

_____

What is your biggest concern about communicating this message?

_____

_____

_____

What is important to your audience right now? What matters most to them?

_____

_____

_____

What is the roadblock or resistance to your message?

_____

_____

_____

What are the fears and concerns of your audience?

_____

_____

_____

What is at stake for you?

_____

_____

_____

What is at stake for them?

_____

_____

_____

What do they want and need from you?

_____

_____

_____

What do you want and need from them?

_____

_____

_____

What can they expect from you?

_____

_____

_____

What is your call to action?

_____

_____

_____

What is your personal commitment to this? How will you put skin in the game?

_____

_____

_____

What metaphor captures the essence of your message? Start with, "Think of it like this . . ."

_____

_____

_____

Identify three intentions that can guide the delivery of your message. What thoughts and feelings do these intentions address?

1. _____
2. _____
3. _____

Leaders who rest on "I'm the leader, people should do as they're told" cannot maximize their power and influence. Effective influencers are able to inspire, motivate, and persuade others to join them on the journey. All of the people whom you hope to influence will be bringing their own experiences and biases to the table—biases that, if not overcome, could thwart your leadership efforts.

A clear and precise intention, combined with thoughtful and figurative language, can position you to be at your most persuasive and influential.

11

THE ART OF
LEADING CHANGE

*Leadership is about change. It's about taking people from
where they are now to where they need to be. The best way to get
people to venture into unknown terrain is to make it
desirable by taking them there in their imaginations.*
—NOEL TICHY

Due to the immense complexity of many organizations, leading change can seem like (and often is) an insurmountable challenge. If one is to be successful in leading change, there are two aspects that are critical to understand. Both are obvious and diametrically opposed. The first is that *change is fundamental to nature and to life*. Everything has a beginning, a middle, and an end. The second is that *change hurts* because we all crave stability and predictability.

With these facts in mind, we can understand that change happens on four levels.

- **Personally**—change in our individual approach and mindset.
- **Interpersonally**—change in relationship with others.
- **Organizationally**—change in relationship to groups in the entire system.
- **Societally**—change in relationship to the larger ecosystem within which our organization exists.

For a leader, it is important to reflect upon and address each of these levels in their decisions and strategic communications. In this chapter, I will share with you several examples of how leaders have stepped into the role of the leader of culture and have used narrative to pave the way for change.

LEADING CHANGE THROUGH NARRATIVE

The first job of the cultural protagonist and chief meaning maker is to dig into your organization's history and seek out the most powerful narratives of change, resilience, innovation, and leadership—find your organization's story.

As I started my company, Protagonist Consulting Group, I was fortunate to connect with Paul Bottino, founder of the Technology and Entrepreneurship Center at Harvard's School of Engineering. Together we discussed how a leader can leverage the power of story to guide innovation within an organization. His explanation serves as a solid narrative framework for leading change through creating meaning.

> **Then.** The leader must first remind others of their heritage. Leaders do this by unearthing and sharing success stories of the past. Where and who were we? What were we known for? What vision did we have for ourselves? What obstacles did we have to overcome to achieve success? The listeners will recognize themselves in the story and be drawn in. This allows them to celebrate their finest attributes and achievements.
>
> **Now.** The leader must discover and make sense of the stories of the confusing present. These reside within the people of the organization who are in touch with its customers. What has changed, or what big event has occurred? What is being asked of us now? What are we known for now? The leader must collect, interpret, synthesize, and validate these stories for the rest of the organization. These stories include a vivid picture of what could be, as well as the challenges that must be overcome to achieve it.
>
> **Next.** The leader must then tell the story of the innovative future. What do we want to be known for? Are our current beliefs, attitudes, and ways of doing things adequate to handle the path forward? What attributes must we embody in order to meet and exceed the new challenges? This story ties back to the spirit of the organization's beginnings and models the new behaviors necessary for success.

Abraham Lincoln's Gettysburg Address followed the storytelling structure Paul describes above. Paul simply applied it to innovation. This is exactly what you can do. Take a look at the resources listed in the endnotes for inspiration.[1] At the end of this chapter you will find a short exercise that you can follow for yourself.

ENABLING QUICK ADOPTION OF
A NEW WAY OF WORKING

One of my coaching clients, Amir Arooni, has a passion for change management. Amir is the CIO at NN Group, a leading Dutch bank and insurance company. I heard the following story first from one of the members of his team as being a powerful, memorable, and successful tool to guide change.

Amir is a highly reflective and relational leader, passionate on the topic of "building learning organizations." He understands his role to be not only the strategic leader but also as a leader of culture. For him, culture is everything. He received a report letting him know that the new way of working, changing from a silo-based process (Waterfall) to a highly collaborative and transparent process (AGILE), was not being adopted. He knew he needed to find a way to create momentum. He took the time to reflect on the situation and soon realized that many people were stuck on the nuances and differences of the new system, rather than just trying to learn it. When it comes to competitive advantage, learning and becoming a learning organization are key, and the facilitation of learning becomes one of the core competencies of management. There are many ways organizations can learn.

> *When it comes to competitive advantage, the facilitation of learning becomes one of the core competencies of management.*
> —AMIR AROONI

As soon as he made this connection, it triggered a recent memory of his daughter's process for learning piano. She did this through the Suzuki method. He then realized that he needed to create a system for his team that would guide their learning and make it easy for them to adopt the new platform.

Amir created a presentation that he delivered to his entire team. He shared his observations about the lack of adoption and a need for a different approach. He shared his insight about his daughter's process for learning the piano, and painted a picture of his vision for using it to guide their learning process. In addition, Amir shared his view on personal mastery and mental models.

The Suzuki method is based on the principles of language acquisition. These include parent responsibility, listening, constant repetition, and encouragement, all of which create a positive flow around learning and adaptation. The Suzuki method is also based on "every child can learn," with the involvement of parents, listening, and repetition. As when a child learns to talk, parents are involved in the musical education learning of their child. In this case, Amir identified the manager as the substitute for the parent. The managers, he argued, could get involved in the process of learning along with their team members. They could learn something before their team members did so they would understand the expectations.

Managers would be responsible for both creating an enjoyable learning environment for their team members, as well as encouraging and coaching them along the way.

Children learn words after hearing them spoken hundreds of times by others. Listening to music every day is important, especially listening to pieces in the Suzuki repertoire. In Amir's case, listening referred to becoming familiar with the new way of working across all IT platforms. For the team member, this meant spending a certain amount of time understanding the new technology from a variety of sources, including webinars, talks, and informal gatherings.

Repetition is exactly as it sounds. Children don't learn a word or piece of music and then discard it. Each element serves as a foundation for the next, more complex element. The team members needed to dig in to the change (the new IT platform and new way of working together) right away. They needed to build a foundation and vocabulary, and then gradually learn to use it in new and more sophisticated ways.

Amir's idea was embraced by managers—and it worked. So we need to ask is, why? I believe that the managers needed a bridge to walk over between the old and the new way of working, thinking, and relating. The Suzuki methodology became that bridge because it contained a number of key ingredients including the following:

- The story that Amir used created a visual impression for everyone that was personal and engaging. He grabbed their attention and opened them up to his idea.

- The analogy was relevant and meaningful. It made sense, established a clear path, was memorable, and was easy to reference and explain to others.

In the end, the Suzuki method served as a system of learning for the entire organization and effectively facilitated the adoption of the new platform.

Look into Your Own Experience

Can you see how looking into other parts of our lives gives us a wealth of information from which we can create compelling narratives?

What are you currently struggling with in your organization?

_____

_____

_____

What parts of your life might you examine to discover new and innovative solutions for these issues?

_____

_____

_____

WHY, HOW, WHAT

As Simon Sinek, author of *Start with Why*, most eloquently posed, "People don't buy *what* you do, they buy *why* you do it."

In an article that I wrote with James Parker, visiting faculty at Rotterdam School of Management, Erasmus University, and co-founder of Parma Consulting Group, we compared the role of the CEO to that of a film director. We looked at the classic film *The Godfather*, which was directed by Francis Ford Coppola and starred Marlon Brando. In this analysis, it is clear that the leader needs to have a clear vision for what he or she wants to create, as well as the capability to share this story with others in a way that is passionate and compelling.

We are convinced that the secret to managing complexity (in film as in business) lies in understanding the connection between vision, strategy, and action or, more simply, to combine the "why," the "how," and the "what." All three elements are needed and have to be balanced and integrated to create a great production.

Why

Coppola's first challenge was to win the hearts of his players, and above all that of Brando, over to his own artistic vision for the film. Brando was a champion of the disenfranchised. He devoted much of his time working for causes such as American Indian rights. *The Godfather* was a deep and extended meditation on power as filtered through the process and culture of American capitalism. This appealed deeply to Brando and was the essential bridge that Coppola used to enlist Brando in his vision.

He also had to find the right balance between imposing an authoritarian prescription and engaging the creative forces of his team in finding a collective vision that they all could own. Every leader has to strike this balance, some in a more directive way than others.

How

He then had to define and communicate the broad strategy for realizing this vision. Again, there is no general rule about how participative or directive this process should be, as it is always dependent on the nature of the leader and qualities of the team. But to work effectively, every member of the cast and crew needed a clear understanding of the broad strategic guidelines for the film.

What

Lastly, he had to design every individual scene in such a way as to get the most out of his players. Each director creates his own style, some highly directive of every aspect of the performance while others allow more latitude to the actors to interpret the roles themselves. But every single member of the cast and crew, from the star to the last name on the long list of functions at the end of the film, has to know the purpose of their actions. As I explained in the article:

> Indeed, it is the ability to diagnose at which of the three levels to focus that distinguishes great directors and, we would argue, great business leaders. Directors such as Coppola hold an integrated view of all three levels and seem to know instinctively at which level to act at any given moment in order to re-energize and to redirect efforts towards the shared goal. This may be at the individual

or collective level. But the key lies in judging whether a disagreement or misunderstanding at the "what" level has its roots in the "how" or the "why," or whether it is just a technical issue. A cast or a business team will swiftly be weary of a leader who constantly and superfluously reminds them of the "why" when they are just trying to get things done. But to focus at the level of tasks when the root of the problem lies in a misunderstanding or miscommunication at another level is to invite failure. An inspiring director will fine tune the corrections at each level to ensure that every cast member knows not only what they have to do, but why and how. As the project progresses, the balance between these three levels will change. The successful leader will be constantly watching the behavior of the team and directing their own interventions at the level dictated by their needs.

VISION AND STRATEGY TO ACTION

While managing client relationships for Harvard Business School for over a decade, I was invited to sit in on a number of iconic business cases. One of my favorites was on Jan Carlzon, president of Scandinavian Airlines, as profiled in his book *Moments of Truth*.

Have a Vision for Yourself as a Leader

Carlzon was a turnaround artist. This was his gift. It was his personal mission to reposition the struggling airline in the market and restore it to profitability. He first needed to have a personal vision for himself as a leader. Carlzon explained:

> The company was not asking me to make all the decisions on my own, only to create the right atmosphere, the right conditions for others to do their jobs better. I began to understand the difference between a traditional corporate executive, who issues instruction after instruction from the top, and the new corporate leader, who must set the tone and keep the big picture in mind.
>
> I also learned why our people started working so wholeheartedly. I think it was because they understood our goals and strategies.

We communicated a vision of what the company could be, and they were willing to take responsibility for making it work.

I could no longer be an isolated and autocratic decision-maker. Instead, I must be a visionary, a strategist, an informer, a teacher, and an inspirer.[2]

Understanding Mission: What Do You Do?

Mission is the nuts and bolts of what you do. These are your personal or the organization's gifts, talents, and capabilities. For SAS airlines, its mission was simple: to transport people and their belongings by air.

Clarifying Vision: Who Do You Want Your Organization to Be, to Whom, by When?

Upon entering into the organization, Carlzon asked the simple question, "What is your vision for the organization?" The senior leaders answered, "To be the best airline in the world."

To which he thought, "That is like trying to cure world hunger." It was noble, but not specific enough. You cannot build a strategy for that because it is unachievable.

He then shifted a bit, asking, "When are you at your best? When do you feel the most purposeful, satisfied, and fulfilled?"

To which leaders answered, "When we serve the frequent business traveler. Short legs of travel with people that we get to know and with whom we build a relationship."

"Great, let's then align our vision with our gifts and refine it. To be the best airline in the world, serving the frequent business traveler." To him and everyone in the organization this vision held deep meaning and a sense of purpose.

Establishing Strategy: How Will You Get There?

Once a specific vision was created, Carlzon could dive in deeper and look for the critical pathways to achieving it.

Carlzon realized that the first 15-second encounter between a passenger and the frontline people, from ticket agent to flight attendant, sets the tone of the entire company in the mind of the customer. This is what Carlzon calls the "moment of truth":

If we are truly dedicated to orienting our company toward each customer's individual needs, then we cannot rely on rule books and instructions from distant corporate offices. We have to place responsibility for ideas, decisions, and actions with the people who *are* SAS during those 15 seconds: ticket agents, flight attendants, baggage handlers, and all the other frontline employees. If they have to go up the organizational chain of command for a decision on an individual problem, then those 15 golden seconds will elapse without a response, and we will have lost an opportunity to earn a loyal customer.[3]

Guiding Action: Making Execution Meaningful

Together with his team Carlzon identified about five strategic priorities that would guide the actions of the organization. Two are profiled below.

Strategy #1: Drive Decision-Making Down the Line

The first was to drive decision-making down to the line. If the "15-second" encounter was to be followed, then if a problem arose with a frequent business traveling passenger, it was not productive for the agent to fill out a form, send it to middle management, and then have a decision made in three weeks to take care of the passenger. In that scenario, the disgruntled business traveler would have already changed her preferred airlines.

No, they needed to put the decision-making responsibility in the hands of the agent so that they could take care of the passenger on the spot. This would do two essential things. One, it would retain the passenger and actually increase their brand loyalty. Second, it would create a sense of meaning and purpose for the gate agent. Being empowered to make decisions helps employees better perceive themselves as "owning" the company's mission. Recall the stories we tell ourselves, and contrast "my company has a grand mission, but I'm only a faceless cog in it" with "as a gate agent, I have the power to help my customers have a better flight." A virtuous cycle.

Strategy #2: Utilize the Efficient Fleet of Regional Jets

The second strategy that was important to achieving the company's vision was to utilize the most efficient fleet of regional jets. Carlzon noticed that there was a reluctance to sell off four new transatlantic planes. He needed a way to reposition his team on this decision.

Much like the director of a play or movie, Carlzon engineered or "staged" a moment where he and his team were standing in front of a wall of glass windows with the four gleaming planes in full view. He turned to admire the planes and mentioned to his team how beautiful they were. To which they replied, "Yes, they are the pride of our fleet." He then casually asked how much money was wrapped in these beautiful planes. The number they gave to him was staggering. He then asked if the planes were being used, which they were not because of the new vision and strategy. The team took a pause and collectively realized the need to sell them.

Carlzon did not have to be the "bad guy" and issue an order for the planes to be sold. Because he and the team had established a clear vision and strategy, he only had to lead them back to a place where they were reconnected to the "why."

NOW IT'S YOUR TURN

Please use the following two exercises to craft your vision and strategy and communicate them to key stakeholders.

Crafting Your Vision and Strategy

Begin this process by clearly articulating your organization's mission, purpose, vision, and strategy. Answer the questions in the following template.

Mission

- In plain words, explain exactly what you do. Include basics such as the services you provide and products you offer.

Purpose

- Why do you do this?
- Why is the work that you do meaningful and significant to you?
- Why is the work that you do meaningful and significant to your customers?
- Why is the work that you do meaningful and significant to society?

Vision

- Who do you want to be? What is your purposeful goal?
- Who are your targeted customers?
- What is a reasonable time frame to accomplish your goal?

Strategy

- How will you get there?

- What are your top three to five strategic priorities that would get you to your goal?

Communicating Your Vision and Strategy to Key Stakeholders

How do you communicate your vision and strategy to key stakeholder groups? By ensuring that all of the actions you take in your organization are strategic and meaningful. In order to do this, you must first clarify your own mission and goals by using the empathy map shown in Figure 11.1 and be as specific as possible.

Think about an upcoming message that you need to communicate. Identify a specific stakeholder group that you need to deliver it to and answer the questions in the empathy map. Draw the map out on a flipchart and work on it standing up with a colleague or your team. Typical stakeholders include employees, customers, shareholders, and the wider society.

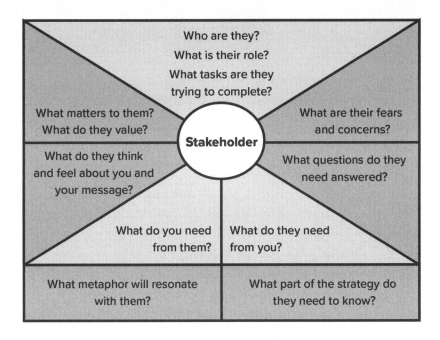

FIGURE 11.1 **Stakeholder empathy map**

Now, use the narrative framework from the beginning of the chapter to tailor your message.

Then (Past)

- Who were we?
- What was important to us?
- What were we known for?

Now (Present)

- Who are we now?
- What has happened?
- What has changed?
- How has this affected us?
- What is important to us now?

Next (Future)

- Where are we going, and why?
- What is inspiring about this future?
- What challenges lie ahead?
- Who do we need to be, what do we need to learn to meet these challenges?
- Why am I committed to going there?
- Why should we be committed to going there?

Finally, begin to craft your message by using the following prompts as launch points:

Headline message: "Why are we here?"

_____

_____

_____

Now, look at the message you crafted and think about how you can meet your audience where they are. Acknowledge their thoughts and feelings and incorporate ways you can connect to what is important to them.

_____

_____

_____

Based on the work you have already done, construct your narrative.
Try possible narrative frameworks: Using the Past, Present, and Future framework allows you to paint an aspirational vision. Using the Story of Self, Story of Us, and Story of Now framework allows you to galvanize your audience around a particular challenge.

_____

_____

_____

Create a meaningful metaphor. Start with the following: Think of us (it) like this . . .

_____

_____

_____

Identity your call to action by answering "Why now?"

_____

_____

_____

The narrative forms in this chapter are powerful in that they enable you to create meaningful action. They also demonstrate how one story, one presentation, or one approach won't fit all situations. You have to _step back_ and get a firm handle on the problem that is in front of you. These structures will allow you to create the momentum you're looking for.

THE ART OF MAKING
GREAT PRESENTATIONS

A good speech is like a pencil; it has to have a point.
—AUTHOR UNKNOWN

A s every leader knows, making presentations is an important part of a leader's role. There is an expectation that, as a leader, you are a confident and competent public speaker. But how often is this the case? How many times do we see a leader step up behind a podium and deliver a factual but boring speech? Is it that leaders overestimate their capabilities? Are they not aware of the impact that they are having on their audience? Is it that they do not see the value of taking the time to prepare and rehearse?

In this chapter, I will share with you one of my most memorable moments in front of an audience, as well as some of my favorite coaching engagements with individuals on highly visible and critical presentations. From these stories, I will identify a few key principles and practices in both preparation and delivery that you can take away and put into action immediately.

As a performing artist, I have learned to build an open and honest connection with my audience. My purpose as a performer was to lift my audience out of their day-to-day worries for an hour or so, and for them to feel what it was like to let go and play. It was my strategy to involve my audience to the point where they became not only invested audience members, but a willing and integral part of the performance. We created the final product together.

STEPPING BACK INTO THE FIRE

It was October 1999 and I was working at Boston University. This was my transitional job between being a full-time performer and leaping into the world of corporate learning. My role was as a rehabilitation counselor and career coach for people with emotional disabilities. At the same time, I was getting my master's in business administration, delivering corporate training programs across campus, and doing some occasional performing gigs on the weekends. Most of my days involved sitting in a chair and talking. This was a big transition from being a full-time performing artist.

One day I got a call from an old performing friend, Tony. He said that he was organizing a holiday show for a large corporate client, 2,500 people, and that they were interested in having a wire walker kick off the show. He said to me, "This is what you do, right?"

I paused for a second to take in exactly what he was asking and then replied, "Yes, that's right!"

"Great!" he said. "Are you interested?"

In what felt like an eternity, I had a massive inner dialogue. On the one hand it had been almost five years since I had wire walked. I said to myself, "Are you crazy?" On the other hand, I desperately missed the excitement and energy of being in front of a large audience. In my mind I said, "I know how to do this. I can do this." And before I knew it I replied, "Yes!" He said, "Great! How much would you charge?"

This is where it got difficult. I had to put the price up high enough to make it worth it, and that if they said no, I would not be disappointed. Maybe even relieved! He said, "That's a lot of money, but I will ask them. I'll give you a call tomorrow."

The next day Tony called and let me know that the client had accepted my offer. In that moment I experienced a blast of excitement, but also felt a small bead of sweat form on my forehead. This was no easy task I had accepted. I had two months to prepare myself for the show. A full eight weeks. I knew what I needed to do and immediately created a plan of action. Two days a week I was in the gym doing mostly leg lifts. Two other days a week I went across the street to the theater department to a small room that had pins in the walls specifically designed to rig up a wire. This is where I had first learned my craft and where I felt very comfortable.

Four weeks into the process I realized I was in trouble. My legs were getting stronger and I felt good at the lower height, but I just could not get my balance and confidence at the seven-foot level. I sat down for a moment and had to figure out a way to get this done. Quitting was not an option.

After a few minutes, I knew what I needed to do. I needed to ask for help. So I called my old friend, Bill Finlay, at Union College in upstate New York and told him about my predicament. He laughed and told me to pack up my car with all of my equipment and get up there. He said to me, "Don't worry, we will get this thing done!" That immediately gave me a sense of relief and confidence. I packed up the car and drove four hours to Saratoga Springs ready for a very long weekend.

As soon as I got to his theater, we put up the wire rig and began working. His coaching and prompting were just what I needed. On the first day, he grounded me in the basics. It felt good to be working together again. On the second day he guided me back into a place of balance and confidence. I regained the sense of freedom that I once felt on the wire, but had lost. I was fully energized, and my creativity started to flow. We brainstormed all sorts of different crosses and tricks, but in the end, reduced the routine to five passes across the wire. Each one increased in complexity and difficulty, but all were well within my range of comfort.

He then repeated his most important principle. *It's not about the skill, it's about your audience.* What do you want this performance to be about? What do you want your audience to feel or do? We agreed that the best approach would be the most straightforward, to excite and rouse the audience. Together we came up with a French chef character who would engage with the audience and share his excitement of the culinary experience through the metaphor of the wire.

The three days went by very quickly. As I drove back home, I felt confident in both my abilities and plan of action.

It was the evening of the event, and I was standing next to my fully assembled wire rig, which was sparkling from the lights that shone down from the ceiling. The audience had just finished their dinner, and the noise level was starting to build. Being the opening act, I was anxious and excited.

Then, two minutes before I was to perform, I experienced what I could only call a feeling of dread. All of the color went out of my face, and I broke out into a cold sweat. This was not good. I started to see images of myself falling off the wire. Fortunately, Bill and I had practiced in case something like this happened. I took a deep breath and literally shook off my fear. I took another breath and pictured myself standing tall and free on the wire. All of the color came back into my face, and I reconnected with my sense of purpose. Tony gave me a big introduction, the audience cheered, and I made my entrance.

All I can say is that this was one of my best and favorite performances of my career. I felt solid and playful in my routines and totally connected to my audience. They loved my French chef character. At the end of the performance I did my orchestrated dismount and extended my arms to the cheers, laughter, and applause of my audience. I walked back to the spot where I had begun, turned to face the audience once more, took a deep breath, and let it go.

When I look back on this event, it always brings me a sense of accomplishment. It was the button on my performing career. I took away some solid lessons that I will carry with me always.

The routine itself was only 10 minutes long, but I can safely estimate that I spent well over 80 hours of rehearsal time preparing for it. Yes, it was a huge hill to climb, but that is what was needed for this particular project. These are my takeaways:

- Have a goal and a sense of purpose. Know why you are doing it.
- Create a well-structured plan and stick to it.
- Bring a sense of discipline, experience, creativity, and humility to the work.
- Know when to ask for help.
- Practice resilience and have a plan for emotional sinkholes.
- Breathe.
- Have a big vision for what you want to do, but boil it down to something essential and achievable without losing the sense of excitement.
- It's all about your audience.
- Find the sense of freedom in the activity.

PREPARATION, COMMITMENT, AND LEADERSHIP

Just this fall I had the pleasure of coaching Darryl Fess, president of Brookline Bank, a regional community bank in the Boston area, in preparation for a keynote speech he was to make to a group of 500 credit risk officers. This was far and away the most significant speech he had ever made, and he wanted to get it right. But he had no idea how much time, effort, preparation, rehearsal, and commitment it would take to get there. The good news: he was up for the challenge and he totally nailed it.

Darryl had never worked with a coach before and was appropriately cautious. On our initial call I asked him to tell me about the event, what his goals were for the presentation, and why he had accepted the invitation. He said that being his first year as president it was important for him to have a presence in the banking community.

There were six weeks before the presentation and, given what I then knew after getting to know Darryl, I laid out a plan that I felt confident would allow him to achieve his goals. He accepted it and we went to work. We ended up meeting five times in person and at least another six times on the phone. Our coaching covered the contextual flow of his presentation, the crafting of his opening, and some of the key concepts he wanted to cover. We worked on various exercises to enhance his physical presence and vocal flexibility. This included him choosing a movie monologue that he practiced and presented to me. I also had him share with me a recent personal experience that we could use to practice direct narrative storytelling skills.

I have to say that throughout this entire process, Darryl was open, willing, and committed. I challenged him in numerous ways to expand way beyond his physical and vocal comfort zone. He stayed with me. I also challenged him to understand what it meant to open himself up to his audience and be fully present and vulnerable. He stayed with me. I was relentless on getting him to bring his personal story to life with every sensory detail, feeling, and gesture. He stayed with me.

We were about three weeks into the process when we hit a turning point. I had done some work recrafting his opening remarks to be more succinct, but it just wasn't doing it for me. It went like this:

> Thank you for having me as a keynote at your Management Association meeting. I especially want to thank my colleague who gave me this opportunity to represent the community bank perspective, as well as many employees of my bank who have endured my efforts to prepare for this event.

I looked up from my notes and said, "Darryl, I would like you to consider making a change to your opening. It is flat and will not grab the attention of the audience. I would like you to consider using your story as the opener." He looked back at me without saying a word. I could see that he was not taking this idea well. He had just spent the last week memorizing the opening, and now I wanted him to change direction?

181

I made my case that he needed something to grab the attention of his audience right at the top of his speech, and that there was no better way than with a story. He instinctively knew it was the right play, and I saw him valiantly fight his urge to resist. He saw the hill that he needed to climb, and he accepted the challenge. He started telling his story over and over to his wife and kids. He told his story to his colleagues and employees. He even reserved the stage in the theater across the street from his office to rehearse in front of a group of willing employees. He enlisted their support and asked for their feedback. It was not easy, but he began to get it. We then realized that his story had a perfect lead-in to his presentation. It had a clear and relevant point that would tie into his speech.

The story described a recent business trip to Nashville. His wife had joined him. After seeing a concert at the Grand Ole Opry, they were returning to their hotel, which was in the center of the city. The streets were teaming with people. They decided to go to an Italian restaurant rather than eat another meal of barbeque. The restaurant was a bit dingy, there was rock and roll playing on the jukebox, and the red vinyl booths were covered in duct tape. It was definitely not what they had expected, but it was full of people, so how bad could it be? They decided to play it safe and order a pizza that, when it came, was atrocious. He then said, "The pizza wasn't good, but we ate it, and we didn't get sick. It was an acceptable risk. And this is what I would like to talk with you about tonight. Community banking is all about assessing acceptable risk." Bam!

There were two other key elements to his presentation that are worth noting.

- **Get out from behind the podium.** I did not want Darryl to stand behind the podium for this presentation. However, it was a 45-minute speech and way too much to memorize. So, I had an idea for him to use a music stand. He would carry the music stand out, place it on the floor, and put his binder on it.

- **Practice with props.** In our last rehearsal I saw that it was awkward for him to carry out the music stand and the binder. My background was in new vaudeville theater, and working with props was a critical part of any performance. So, we rehearsed his entrance. He practiced how he carried the two items onto the stage, how he placed the stand on the ground, and how he opened and placed the binder onto the stand.

- **Pause before you start.** It was important for him to practice pausing before he started to speak. He looked out at the audience and took a breath.

This sense of timing conveys large amounts of confidence to any audience. As Mark Twain once said, "The right word may be effective, but no word was ever as effective as the rightly timed pause."

- **Lead with a story.** The first words that he spoke were, "It's three weeks ago and my wife and I are getting out of a cab in downtown Nashville ..." He was off to the races.

- **Speak to be heard.** Darryl had a tendency to be a bit soft-spoken. We wanted to make sure that he was conscious about this. He had something important to say, and it was his job to make sure that every person in that room heard him.

  What happened here? Darryl told me afterward that the audience was spellbound when he carried the music stand onto the stage. One of his colleagues, who was a musician, said the opening moment was a delight and grabbed the attention of the audience right away. Also, his story was on the mark and set the tone for the entire speech.

- **Involve your audience.** Darryl's initial view of his speech, like so many keynotes, was a one-way communication. Rarely do you see a keynote presenter actually involve the audience and draw them into either a conversation or active thought process. This is what I invited Darryl to consider. How could he get his audience thinking along with him on a key topic he wanted to introduce? After some discussion, we came up with the idea to present the audience with a case study. Put them in the role to evaluate a critical business decision. The topic was on the business impact of disruptive technologies. He liked the idea, but the actual process of introducing the interactive format with his audience proved to be more difficult. Below is a list of the steps that we worked on.

  - Tee up what he was going to do in a clear and concise manner.
  - Describe the role he wanted his audience to play.
  - Outline the case and the decision to be made.
  - Ask them to turn to the person in the next seat and discuss the decision.
  - Report out their insights and findings.

It took many iterations before he got it right. He discussed it and tried it out on a number of people before settling on the right script, process, and delivery style. It worked. Not only did he tee up the concept well, but the activity gave life to his presentation at just the spot where people got a little restless.

He received compliments from many people over the next week or so. This bolstered his confidence and stayed with him.

The following week, Darryl had to make a short, informal introduction at a reception. The year before, at this same reception, he never gave the presentation a moment of thought or preparation. He remembered trying to get people's attention and finishing his remarks before many in the room even noticed he was there.

This time, he made sure to get an introduction. He stepped into the middle of the room and took several deep breaths. He waited patiently until the entire room was quiet and he had everyone's attention before giving his remarks. He lifted his arms out with a generous gesture and made sure that his voice was slow, loud, and clear so that everyone in the room could hear him. The feedback that he received was, again, very reinforcing.

LEAD BETWEEN THE LINES— IT'S DOABLE!

Have you ever had to make a presentation where your entire speech was written by someone else? You might have had the opportunity to add some things, but the script was done and all you needed to do was to read it. How much fun was that?

Several years ago, I was flown to Montreux, Switzerland, to coach the CEO of a large beverage company and his top team on their annual town hall presentations. The morning I arrived I met an interesting guy named Aarush. Right off the bat I liked him. He had a good laugh and a funny sense of humor.

That afternoon I was to sit in an empty room and watch all 10 presentations that were to be made the following day. I had 10 to 15 minutes with each speaker to help them in any way that I could. As I was about to sit down, someone asked if I was going to coach Aarush. To which I replied, "Yes." He rolled his eyes and said to me, "Good luck!"

When it was Aarush's turn, he stood behind the podium and in a quiet voice read his speech word for word. He never took his eyes off of the page. The slides that he showed were unreadable even from the front row. I knew this was going to be a tough one.

When he arrived at the room where I was doing my coaching we greeted each other warmly. He sat down and I said, "Aarush, I saw your presentation.

Your slides looked amazing. I could not read anything on them, but the colors were excellent." He started to laugh.

I then asked him, "What is the one thing that you want your audience to walk away with?" (He was pitching the idea of putting a bottling plant in eastern Europe.) He said in his pleasant Indian voice, "That it is doable!"

"Great," I said. "What I want you to do is to read the first few lines of your script. Then, pause. Look up and point to one person in the audience. Look at this person right in the eyes and say the following... 'What I want you to know is that this is doable!'... can you do this?"

He said, "Yes, of course." We practiced it a bit until he felt comfortable. I then suggested that he repeat this several other times throughout his speech and to do it differently every time. He laughed. We shook hands, and that was it.

The next day I was standing in the back of the auditorium watching the presentations when Aarush stepped to the podium. I was energized and eager to see how he was going to do. He started and read the first paragraph, then looked up and, in a soft voice, said the words, "It is doable."

Not exactly as we had planned. I immediately slumped and let out an audible sigh. In an instant, he perked up and said, "Now, my coach in the back of the room would have wanted me to say those words like Robert De Niro, IT'S DOABLE! But I want to say them like this . . ." and he repeated the words in his Indian dialect.

He finished with a flourish, saying, "But what I really want you to know about this project is, "It's Doable!" Everyone laughed. He broke through to his audience and made a solid connection. He then repeated it several times in funny ways. My favorite was when he brought his team of four up to the stage in chorus line fashion and said, "What is it, guys?" To which they replied while leaning in formation, "It is doable."

If you have a prewritten script, the lessons are as follows:

- **Prepare your key point.** What is the one thing that you want your audience to walk away and remember?

- **Connect with your audience.** Once in a while, stop and look directly at someone in your audience and let that person know what you want them to remember.

- **Let your personality come through.** Aarush was a smart and funny person. He just needed permission to let it out.

PRESENTATIONS ARE YOUR
PERSONAL PROVING GROUNDS

It is no wonder that studies have shown that the fear of public speaking is greater than our fear of death. Public speaking has the potential of playing to one of our deepest fears, rejection. Upon examination, when we walk up in front of any group, no matter if they are known or unknown, there are many destructive thoughts and feelings lurking in the wings.

> When faced with standing up in front of a group, we break out into a sweat because we are afraid of rejection. And at a primal level, the fear is so great because we are not merely afraid of being embarrassed, or judged. We are afraid of being rejected from the social group, ostracized and left to defend ourselves all on our own. We fear ostracism still so much today it seems, fearing it more than death, because not so long ago getting kicked out of the group probably really was a death sentence.[1]

If you think about my wire walking story at the beginning of this chapter, this is what I experienced in the last two minutes before my performance. All sorts of negative visual images came into my mind causing the physiological experience of dread. The good news is, as we explored in many of the chapters of this book, we can plan for these moments, anticipate failure, and train our minds and bodies to respond positively. And, as I experienced, we quickly regather our forces and achieve excellence.

I invite you to see any presentation, whether large or small, as a Trial by Fire. See public speaking engagements as opportunities to step into your Best Self. Each success will build upon the last. Take the time to use the tools provided in this book to be well prepared. Become deeply familiar with not only "what" you want to communicate, but "why" it is important to you, and then think about "why" it might be important to your audience. Give your audience something to think about, experience, and act upon.

Before any presentation, be sure to get to the room early and work out the technical details. Become familiar with the space. Practice your entrance. Rehearse how you will step onto the stage, how you will look out into the audience, and how you will project a positive and welcoming presence. Remember, your audience wants you to be successful. If you are, then their time spent listening to you has been well spent, and they will reward you for it with a rousing round of applause!

OPRAH WINFREY AT THE GOLDEN GLOBE AWARDS

I would like to leave you with one shining example of courage, conviction, and humility. It is the Cecil B. DeMille Award acceptance speech by Oprah Winfrey at the 2018 Golden Globe Awards. Her presentation begins with a story.

> In 1964, I was a little girl sitting on the linoleum floor of my mother's house in Milwaukee watching Anne Bancroft present the Oscar for best actor at the 36th Academy Awards. She opened the envelope and said five words that literally made history: "The winner is Sidney Poitier." Up to the stage came the most elegant man I had ever seen. I remember his tie was white, and of course his skin was black, and I had never seen a black man being celebrated like that. I tried many, many times to explain what a moment like that means to a little girl, a kid watching from the cheap seats as my mom came through the door bone-tired from cleaning other people's houses. But all I can do is quote and say that the explanation is in Sidney's performance in *Lilies of the Field*:
>
> Amen, amen, amen, amen.
>
> . . . But it's not just a story affecting the entertainment industry. It's one that transcends any culture, geography, race, religion, politics, or workplace. So I want tonight to express gratitude to all the women who have endured years of abuse and assault because they, like my mother, had children to feed and bills to pay and dreams to pursue. They're the women whose names we'll never know. They are domestic workers and farm workers. They are working in factories, and they work in restaurants, and they're in academia, engineering, medicine, and science. They're part of the world of tech and politics and business. They're our athletes in the Olympics and they're our soldiers in the military.[2]

In her short and powerful speech, Oprah Winfrey was present, open, and fully engaged her audience. Her voice was strong, confident, and inviting. Her cadence was melodic. She spoke not only for herself, but for all of us. Her story was our story.

13

THE ART OF CREATING A
LEARNING ORGANIZATION

*A learning organization is a place where people continually
expand their capacity to create the results they truly desire,
where new and expansive patterns of thinking are nurtured,
where collective aspiration is set free, and where people
are continually learning how to learn together.*
—PETER SENGE

For those of you who aspire to create healthier and more effective teams
and organizations, it is crucial to look outside of your business domain for
clues to new ideas, approaches, and archetypes that will assist you in achieving your objectives.

In this final chapter, I offer a variety of tools that can be employed to foster
a culture of learning within your team and organization.

ENSEMBLE MINDSET

An ensemble theater company can be an inspirational model for creating a
learning organization. The characteristics and traits of theater ensembles suggest to us new ways of considering what learning means for the individual,
team, and organization. The definition of an ensemble is an approach to acting that aims for a unified effect achieved by all members of a cast working together on behalf of the play, rather than emphasizing individual performances.

The goal is to create a seamless, living world on stage. An ensemble fosters a sense of interconnectivity among its members, and individuals feel a part of something greater than themselves.

I would venture to say this is not much different from how many leaders who aspire to create a culture of learning might describe the vision for their own teams and organizations. Take a look below at the way the Traveling Players, an ensemble group, speaks about the ensemble mindset:

> At its heart, an ensemble prioritizes the success of the whole over the success of the individual. This is in stark contrast to the way theatre often works: an ensemble struggles against the tendency for the "most talented" actors getting the "best parts." Ensemble work challenges both of those ideas by valuing the contributions of every member of the cast and crew.[1]

As many of us have experienced, our organizations tend to focus on recruiting and promoting the best talent. It makes total sense. However, as we will see in research by Google cited later in this chapter, it is not always the groups with the best talent that receive the best results. Here too, as the Traveling Players discuss, the ensemble mindset comes into play:

> [Players are] responsible to the larger group, rather than thinking of their own interests first. . . . Everyone in the group gets what they need. If everyone's focus is in toward the group, they can help, support, encourage, and challenge each other. That way, when problems arise . . . there is enough trust, goodwill, and confidence for the group to sustain itself. . . . In this kind of environment, performers can take greater risks and experience greater growth, knowing that the ensemble will catch them when they fall.[2]

Here again, I think many leaders aspire to build a sense of respect, mutuality, and purpose within their teams. Even in ensemble theater there must be an alignment of both personal and team goals. If the individuals within the team can find this sense of alignment within themselves and feel that the others within the team are equally aligned, then goodwill has the opportunity to flourish among the members, and great results tend to follow.

The Network of Ensemble Theaters modeled the structure of its organization in the image of the theater ensembles that created it. It has an overarching set of principles that guide it—ideas such as shared leadership, giving strength to each other and sharing resources, creating a forum for controversy and debate, and documenting and articulating the heritage and body of work that has been created.

Following are the values that guide the organization.

- Collaboration—two or more people working together toward a shared goal.
- Equity and Inclusion—all voices are heard. All contributions are valued equally.
- Transparency—honesty and open communication. No hidden agendas.
- Excellence—bringing one's Best Self to each and every interaction and performance.
- Respect—admiration for the qualities and abilities of others.
- Active Engagement—full attention, focus, and commitment.
- Knowledge Building—generous and collective sharing of ideas, insights, and experience.[3]

Looking at the principles and values above, are there any that do not apply to a learning culture? Do any of these make you nod your head in agreement? How could you put these into practice with your own team and organization?

Many managers and leaders struggle with their decision-making process. In more hierarchical structures, it is very difficult for leaders to shift from a top-down, command-and-control style of leading and decision-making, to a more inclusive, distributed approach. It takes an internal shift of mindset, role, and identity. If we consider Herminia Ibarra's notion of personal growth that we covered in Chapter 6, we realize that these internal shifts happen as a result of our experiences. It is very difficult to think one's way through these types of transformations. It takes conscious and deliberate action. And the very action itself becomes a living model for learning and leading. It is the relationship between conscious doing and becoming. Let's take a look at how this approach could unleash the collective Best Self of your team.

ARE YOU A TEAM OR A WORKING GROUP?

Learning cultures begin at the top of organizations. The most senior leaders must first engage in a process of building a highly functional team. They need to understand the importance of defining the vision and strategy of the organization and communicate this in an inspiring and purposeful way to their employees. Culture will then spread out within an organization organically, one leader and one group at a time.

The key to unlocking the brilliance in a team lies in understanding the importance of building the relational fabric among the members. A *working group* is a collection of individuals contributing their expertise from their point of view. A *team* is a collection of individuals who share a common purpose and are committed to reaching that goal together.

WHAT ARE YOU A LEADER OF?

What are you a leader of? This is a primary question that I ask many of my coaching clients. For task-driven people, they might say they are a leader of execution. If you aspire to create a learning organization, you need to be a leader of learning.

How does this show up in practice? In a recent *Inc.* magazine article titled "Google Spent 2 Years Studying 180 Teams. The Most Successful Ones Shared These 5 Traits," Michael Schneider highlighted a research study on team effectiveness conducted by Google. It was called Project Aristotle. Specifically, Google wanted to know why some teams excelled while others fell behind.

> Over two years, Google studied 180 teams, conducted 200-plus interviews, and analyzed over 250 different team attributes. Unfortunately, though, there was still no clear pattern of characteristics that could be plugged into a dream-team generating algorithm.
>
> Before this study . . . Google execs believed that building the best teams meant compiling the best people. It makes sense. The best engineer plus an MBA, throw in a PhD, and there you have it. The perfect team, right? In the words of Julia Rozovsky, Google's people analytics manager, "We were dead wrong."[4]

After researching the work of prominent psychologists and sociologists on group norms, collaboration, and collective intelligence, they realized that, indeed, the best teams are not always the ones made up of the superstar performers. Not surprising, diversity among the teams was identified as the critical aspect of creating great teams. The teams needed to be equipped with a range of tools to tackle tough problems and thus be able to optimize their results.

However, it was noted that diversity alone was not the solution. The most telling indicator of high-performing teams was how each of the members felt within the group. This was the collective spirit that unlocked the intelligence and contribution of the diverse members.

They came up with five critical characteristics of the best performing teams.

1. **Dependability.** Team members get things done on time and meet expectations.

2. **Structure and clarity.** High-performing teams have clear goals, and have well-defined roles within the group.

3. **Meaning.** The work has personal significance to each member.

4. **Impact.** The group believes their work is purposeful and positively impacts the greater good.

5. **Psychological Safety.** ... [Everyone on the team feels] safe to take risks, voice their opinions, and ask judgment-free questions.

After reading the article, I had two insights. The first is how similar the traits of Google's high-performing teams were to those of a high-performing theater ensemble. The second is that these traits are not new. They have been known, valued, and practiced in some of the world's most progressive organizations for many years; the difference is that Google has influence across many spheres. When I read this article, I immediately saw its applicability with some of the teams I work with at MIT and with my other clients.

One of my clients was a Boston-based nonprofit organization. Our work together was focused on creating a culture of learning in the organization. I introduced the Google article to the director as a vehicle for engaging the various teams in the organization, and to bring the concept to life.

Rather than just give the article to the teams to read, I incorporated instructional design principles and created an exercise to engage the members and promote learning. The process included a one-page rating sheet on each of the five dimensions. The members of the senior management team followed this process:

1. Hand out the Google article to the members of your team. Ask them to read the article in advance of the next team meeting.

2. At the next meeting open up a discussion about the article and, as a group, discuss each of the five dimensions for creating team effectiveness.

3. Hand out the rating sheet. Ask each person to rate themselves as well as the team on each of the five dimensions from their perspective. A copy of the rating sheet is available for download on my website (www.leadingfromyourbestself.com/resources).

4. Ask each person to report his or her ratings. Have them explain to their team members why they gave each dimension a particular rating.

5. Ask the team to create a composite team score for each of the dimensions.

6. Ask the team to look at the dimension with the lowest score and, as a team, decide how they can work together to raise the score one point. The team is to decide on the period of time that they will work on it.

7. At the next weekly meeting, take 15 minutes to check in about the actions the team has been taking around the chosen dimension.

We discovered the following:

- The members of the teams enjoyed the interactions and conversations.
- They felt that the discussions increased their engagement and created a positive experience.
- The conversations promoted respect, appreciation, and cooperation among team members.
- The discussion itself was a learning activity. Engaging in these types of activities is what it means to be a learning organization.
- They appreciated that the team was leading the process, not the supervisor.
- They appreciated the supervisor creating energy and time for these discussions.

The Most Important Thing That We Learned Was . . .

This simple model and process has the potential to become a centerpiece for team learning for at least half a year. However, it must start from the top. It is critical for senior managers to take this initiative seriously. This is accomplished by following the process for themselves first.

They then need to guide their teams through this process. Team leaders must fully commit to maintaining energy and focus on this activity once it is created and hold their teams accountable. They need to encourage the right behaviors, acknowledge specific effort, congratulate their teams on their progress, and publicly recognize them for their success.

If this does not happen, there is a high risk for increased disengagement and cynicism.

We all know how quickly these types of development activities can lose momentum due to the relentlessness of day-to-day activities. All the more important it is to remind each other of the organizational vision that you are trying to create, pay attention to the results, and hold yourself and your colleagues accountable for maintaining energy in the process.

AFTER ACTION REVIEWS

As discussed in the story above, a key element to sustaining learning is by adopting a mindset for experimentation, iteration, and mastery. People and teams need coaching and guidance in their learning process.

Conducting after action reviews (or debriefings) is a central activity of any learning organization. On the individual level, an after action review creates a continual learning process and can effectively replace or at least augment the yearly performance management process. On the team level, it is a great way to get the group talking, sharing, and improving. The recommendation is to use this process at the end of each project or designated period of time. If conducted with a team, it is important to give each person the opportunity to share his or her thoughts on each of the steps.

Let's use the "From a Potential Lawsuit to a $6 Million Check" case example from Chapter 4 as a reference point for this process.

REFLECTION AND DISCUSSION

Start with the experiences of the team members. Dig for pivotal moments and decision points.

- What was our goal? *To achieve an on time and on budget launch.*
- Did we achieve the goal? *Not right away. It was delayed by six months.*

- What were the moments that mattered? *Having an authentic conversation with the client.*

- What did you see, hear, and feel at these moments? *Relief, excitement, and satisfaction.*

Identify patterns of behavior.

- What actions and behaviors did we utilize that worked? *Self-reflection, thoughtful planning, and an honest conversation.*

- What actions and behaviors did not work? *Earlier in the process, staying in our silos and not reaching out. Blaming the other party.*

- How was our strategy effective? Not effective? *We achieved success by having an authentic conversation with the client. We were able to get on the same page and also align the teams.*

- Knowing what we know now, what would we do differently? *Establish open lines of communication early, pay attention to the disruptive voices, and bring the parties together and discuss the issues on a consistent basis.*

Explore core values and motivations.

- How were our actions aligned with our core values? *Our breakthrough actions were based on open and honest communication.*

- What were the motivations behind our decisions? *Get the platform launched on time and on budget, and maintain the integrity of our work and the client relationship.*

- What were the core assumptions that we used as part of our planning process? *Just do it. We will figure it out.*

- Knowing what we know now, what assumptions do we need to change? *Building relationship first enables quicker resolution of issues as they arise.*

Introduce new models, frameworks, and skills.

- What new lens can you introduce to the group to view the issue? *Use communication tools like the Observe-Think-Feel-Want framework*

- What new skills does the team need that will help them fill the gaps?
  - *Ongoing communication skills development.*
  - *Richer team discussions.*
  - *Stronger team leadership.*

Practice skills, strategize, and plan for action.

- Work as a team to discuss applications and approaches. *Share best practice stories over scheduled lunches.*
- Find innovative ways to bring the skills to life. *Invite the client into these weekly discussions.*

Move to action.

- Apply insights and skills.
- Make it evidence based.
- Seek feedback.

Figure 13.1 shows this process.

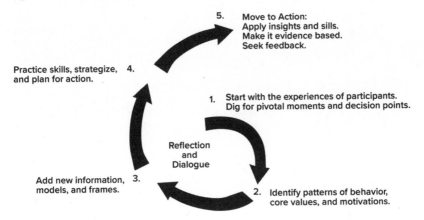

FIGURE 13.1 **After Action Review process**

There are many more activities and tools available that will help you to develop both the cultural mindset and daily practices for becoming a learning organization. The ones provided here will most certainly give you a running start. It happens person by person, team by team. It is when everyone works in concert, like an orchestra or ensemble, that you will discover the melodies and harmonies this approach can yield. I encourage you to look over the principles and values of a theater ensemble, as well as the suggested activities in this chapter, and discuss them with your team. Decide which you could adopt as part of your own process for unleashing your organization's collective Best Self.

FINAL THOUGHTS

Desire is the key to motivation, but it's determination and commitment to an unrelenting pursuit of your goal—a commitment to excellence—that will enable you to attain the success that you seek.
—MARIO ANDRETTI

All the various ideas, concepts, stories, and skills that have been presented in this book have been in service to a central theme of being extraordinary. I encourage you to go back to those chapters that resonated with you the most and try to discover the essential principle behind the idea that was presented. Then look into your own life for how you would best apply that principle. Like an artist, you need to choose your path, learn the value of discipline, and strive for mastery.

In the Preface and Introduction I encouraged you to create a system for learning. In a recent conversation with a coaching client, we were discussing several specific behaviors that he was to practice in service of his overall developmental goal to enhance his socializing skills. I was trying to impress upon him the need to utilize every situation in his life as an experimental laboratory. In the process of communicating this idea to him, the movie *Groundhog Day* came into my mind. If you have not seen the movie, it stars Bill Murray as Phil Connors, a disingenuous television weatherman who gets stranded by a snowstorm in Punxsutawney, Pennsylvania, on February second—Groundhog Day—while filming the famous groundhog, Punxsutawney Phil. Phil (the person) wakes to discover that he is caught in a time loop triggered by his alarm clock that plays the same song, news announcement, and day's activities over and over and over again. He soon realizes that no one else is aware of the day's repetition. No matter what choices he makes on Groundhog Day, his actions have no consequences the next day. At first Phil uses his limitless do-overs to indulge in self-serving behaviors. However, after what seemed like hundreds of iterations, he decides to use the time to better himself and the lives of those around him.

I encouraged my client to engineer his own "Groundhog Day" and put into place a number of weekly situations and actions where he could consciously practice and strive to better himself and the lives of those around him. I shared with him my one-page action planning sheet. You can find this on my website: www.leadingfromyourbestself.com/resources. How could you engineer your own Groundhog Day? Let's take a quick look again at the ideas presented in the book chapter by chapter.

In *Chapter 1* we followed the growth of my friend Hope who reconnected with her experience as a leader in a marching band. She discovered her *Signature Stance*, as well as the inner strength that her early training could give her. By examining the elements of that time in her life she uncovered her keys to being extraordinary.

In *Chapter 2* we explored the signals of presence and identified a few markers that those who project poise and presence possess. We considered the trap of the professional persona and the importance of landing fully inside of ourselves. I encourage you to try out the breathing exercises and build a daily practice to cultivate patience, composure under stress, and a state of positivity, all of which will serve you well in building leadership agility.

In *Chapter 3* we identified ways to find your unique voice. We practiced ways to expand beyond your comfort zone, as well as create an environment that allows others to thrive.

In *Chapter 4* we addressed the reality that the world is not perfect and considered Jerry Seinfeld's approach to dealing with hecklers as a memorable tool to expand into conflict.

In *Chapter 5* we stepped fully into the world of theater and expanded our physical, emotional, and vocal ranges. We learned how to be present and open, as well as how to fix the leaks to our power. We experimented with taking on the *Signature Stances* of many disciplines as a way to find our own spark. I cannot tell you how much I rely on these exercises throughout my day to keep me in the game and be in my Best Self.

In *Chapter 6* we practiced the art of transitioning, from the small moments that we navigate on a daily basis, to the larger transitions that demand a shift of mindset, role, and identity. We learned that making successful transitions in all of the areas of our lives takes reflection and conscious intention, and that all exits are an entrance to somewhere else.

In *Chapter 7* we discovered ways to transition to a new level of relating, and the power of getting to the heart of the matter. And that sometimes our own behavior and drive for results can be the source of our own discomfort.

In *Chapter 8* we dove deep into self-discovery and authenticity. We learned that your story matters and that your true power lies in forming an integrated sense of self and identity. I encourage you to discover, polish, and present those stories that will allow others to "get you."

In *Chapter 9* we covered a lot of ground. We began by stepping onto the path of becoming the leader of culture. We landed fully on the importance of story sharing and meaning making. And we learned what it takes to become an authentic storyteller. I encourage you to start incorporating stories in your daily and strategic communications.

In *Chapter 10* we took a look at influence and the sources of power within organizations. We considered that the development of personal power is the means by which we can create sustained and inspired action in others. We highlighted the use of metaphor and intention as two powerful communication tools useful in enhancing our ability to influence.

In *Chapter 11* we considered the strategic use of metaphor and various narrative structures as critical tools for leading change. I especially appreciated Amir's use of the Suzuki method of teaching piano as a successful means for creating a sustainable system for learning in his organization—and that it came from his ability to self-reflect on his personal experience.

In *Chapter 12* we reviewed several stories illustrating a few key principles and practices in both preparation and delivery of presentations that you can take away and put into action immediately. I encourage you to remember that becoming great at presentations "Is Doable!"

In *Chapter 13* we considered the analogy of the theater ensemble as a framework for a learning organization. I encourage you to explore the world of theater improv to discover how you can bring this idea to life in the daily attitudes and behaviors of your team members.

. . .

Leading from our Best Self begins with adopting a mindset of excellence not perfection. It demands that we stop comparing ourselves with others, which will only lead to arrogance, fear, anxiety, and self-doubt. We learn to displace these detractors by developing self-discipline and a commitment to action. We engage in activities that sharpen our minds, open our hearts, strengthen our bodies, and broaden our spirits. We commit to developing our gifts and talents and learn to put them to the best and highest use. This is how we practice the art of being extraordinary.

This work demands commitment and boldness.

I am reminded of one of my favorite quotes that helps me to step up, step out, and be bold. It is by W. H. Murray:

> Until one is committed, there is hesitancy, the chance to draw back, always ineffectiveness. Concerning all acts of initiative (and creation), there is one elementary truth, the ignorance of which kills countless ideas and splendid plans: that the moment one definitely commits oneself, then Providence moves too. All sorts of things occur to help one that would never otherwise have occurred. A whole stream of events issues from the decision, raising in one's favor all manner of unforeseen incidents and meetings and material assistance, which no man could have dreamed would have come his way.[1]

And another quote from Johann Wolfgang von Goethe:

> Whatever you can do or dream you can, begin it. Boldness has genius, power and magic in it. Begin it now.

We practice the art of being extraordinary when:

- We are Present and Open.
- We land fully and give others our full and undivided attention.
- We Expand into Experience.
- We learn how to transition.
- We Listen with our Eyes!
- We get to the heart of the matter and truly connect authentically with others.
- We drop our guard and allow others to chance to connect with us.
- We slow down to Breathe-Connect-Land before we speak.

- We apply the mindset of an artist and strive for excellence and mastery rather than perfection.
- We engage in acts of kindness and generosity.
- We share our story and listen to the story of others.
- We aspire to be our Best Self.

When we take the time to share what is important to us, what we stand for, what our values are, what we would fight for and give our lives for, only then are we truly able to open ourselves up and discover what is important to others, to know what they stand for, what they value and would fight for, and why it matters so much to them.

Thank you for joining me on this journey to lead from your Best Self. If you want to go beyond this book and continue your leadership development go to: www.leadingfromyourbestself.com/resources. There you will find guided-exercise videos, articles, and other relevant materials to support your learning. I also invite you to connect with me on LinkedIn at www.linkedin.com/in/robsalafia, or reach out to me directly at robsalafia@protagonistconsulting.com to continue this conversation.

At the end of the day, if you pull nothing else from the time that we have spent together, I hope that you will embrace the following principles and practices:

Be Present. Be Bold. Be Vulnerable. Be Authentic. Be Your Best Self.

APPENDIX:
FAVORITE IMAGES

As you know by now, the first half of my career was as a performing artist. During this time I had the extraordinary honor to have been photographed by one of Boston's most renowned photographers, Al Fisher. All of the photographs presented in the following pages are gifts of Linda Fisher in memory of her husband, Al Fisher (1933–2009).

"In Al's beautiful black-and-white studies of Boston street performers," wrote photographer Elin Spring of the exhibit on display at the deCordova Museum, "he 'strove to go beyond the mask to reveal the person at the core underneath,' and in the process captured a delicate balance of both persona and person."[1]

Al Fisher, *The Mime*, 1984; printed 1994, platinum palladium print

Collection of deCordova Sculpture Park and Museum, Lincoln, MA 20108.

Al Fisher, Portrait with boater hat, 1984; silver gelatin print

Al Fisher, Street vendor "Red Nose Mogul," 1984; silver gelatin print

Al Fisher, "Undercover Clown," 1984; silver gelatin print

NOTES

Chapter 1

1. Laura Morgan Roberts et al., "Composing the Reflected Best Self-Portrait: Building Pathways for Becoming Extraordinary in Work Organizations," *Academy of Management Review* 30, no. 4 (October 2005): 712
2. Manuela Heberle, "Ideal Self vs. Real Self: Definition & Difference," Study.com, n.d., accessed April 28, 2018, https://study.com/academy/lesson/ideal-self-vs-real-self-definition-lesson-quiz.html
3. Laura Morgan Roberts et al., "Composing the Reflected Best Self-Portrait," 712.
4. Laura Morgan Roberts et al., "Composing the Reflected Best Self-Portrait," 714

Chapter 2

1. Manuela Heberle, "Ideal Self vs. Real Self: Definition & Difference," Study.com, n.d., accessed April 28, 2018, https://study.com/academy/lesson/ideal-self-vs-real-self-definition-lesson-quiz.html
2. Mareo McCracken, "This Neuroscience Trick Will Help You Overcome Any Fear," *Inc.*, accessed January 29, 2018, https://www.inc.com/mareo-mccracken/this-neuroscience-trick-will-help-you-overcome-any-fear.html.

Chapter 4

1. Brené Brown, *Daring Greatly: How the Courage to Be Vulnerable Transforms the Way We Live, Love, Parent, and Lead* (New York: Portfolio Penguin, 2013), 68.
2. Zuri Davis, "Justin Trudeau Shot Down a Heckler in a Town Hall, and Jerry Seinfeld Actually Responded," Rare Humor, January 24, 2018, https://rare.us/rare-humor/justin-trudeau-shot-down-a-heckler-in-a-town-hall-and-jerry-seinfeld-actually-responded/.
3. Jerry Seinfeld, "Reddit AMA," accessed April 29, 2018, https://www.reddit.com/r/IAmA/comments/1ujvrg/jerry_seinfeld_here_i_will_give_you_an_answer/.

Chapter 5

1. Martha Alderson, "Connecting with Audiences Through Character Emotions," accessed April 28, 2018, https://www.writersstore.com/connecting-with-audiences-through-character-emotions.
2. Melinda Wenner, "Tribulations of a Trial," *Scientific American* 30.301, no. 3, special issue: Understanding Origins (September 2009): 14.
3. William Shakespeare, *Hamlet*, Shakespeare Online, accessed April 28, 2018, http://www.shakespeare-online.com/plays/hamlet_1_3.html.

Chapter 6

1. Herminia Ibarra, *Act Like a Leader, Think Like a Leader* (Boston, Harvard Business Review Press, 2015), 4.
2. Shunryu Suzuki, *Zen Mind, Beginner's Mind* (Colorado: Shambhala Publications, 2005), 2.
3. Robert J. Anderson and William A. Adams. 2016. "Sink or Swim: Setting First-Time Leaders Up for Success." *Chief Learning Officer*, August 31, 2016. http://www.clomedia.com/2016/08/31/sink-or-swim-setting-first-time-leaders-up-for-success/.
4. Interact, *Many Leaders Shrink from Straight Talk with Employees*, February 2016, http://interactauthentically.com/articles/research/many-leaders-shrink-straight-talk-employees/. Report on online survey conducted by Harris Poll on behalf of Interact.

Chapter 7

1. Anna Yusim, "The Importance of Authenticity in Acting and in Life," *Fit for Broadway*, February 21, 2017, http://www.fitforbroadway.com/importance-authenticity-acting-life -emotional-health-anna-yusim-md/.
2. Yusim, "Authenticity."
3. Yusim, "Authenticity."
4. Noel Tichy, *The Cycle of Leadership: How Great Leaders Teach Their Companies to Win* (New York: Harper Business, Reprint edition, 2004), 97.
5. Warren Bennis and Robert J. Thomas, "Crucibles of Leadership." *Harvard Business Review*. Accessed July 28, 2018. https://hbr.org/2002/09/crucibles-of-leadership.
6. Lakshmi Ramarajan, "Past, Present and Future Research on Multiple Identities: Toward an Intrapersonal Network Approach," *The Academy of Management Annals* 8:1, 4

Chapter 9

1. Warren G. Bennis, *On Becoming A Leader*. New York: Basic Books, 2009.

Chapter 11

1. Alison Davis, "To Improve Your Storytelling Skills, Use Abraham Lincoln as Inspiration," February 11, 2018, https://www.inc.com/alison-davis/to-improve-your-storytelling-skills -use-abraham-lincoln-as-inspiration.html.
2. Jan Carlzon, *Moments of Truth* (USA: Ballinger Publishing Company), 8, https://archive.org /stream/momentsoftruth00carl#page/n7/mode/2up/search/create+the+right+atmosphere.
3. Jan Carlzon, *Moments of Truth*, 3

Chapter 12

1. Glenn Croston, "The Thing We Fear More Than Death: Why Predators Are Responsible for Our Fear of Public Speaking," *Psychology Today*, November 29, 2012, https://www .psychologytoday.com/us/blog/the-real-story-risk/201211/the-thing-we-fear-more-death.
2. Oprah Winfrey, "Oprah Winfrey Receives Cecil B. DeMille Award at the 2018 Golden Globes," YouTube video, filmed January 7, 2018, 9:39, posted January 7, 2018, https://www .youtube.com/watch?v=fN5HV79_8B8.

Chapter 13

1. Traveling Players, "What Is an Ensemble?," accessed on April 28, 2018, https:// travelingplayers.org/about/what-is-an-ensemble/.
2. Traveling Players, "What Is an Ensemble?"
3. "Core Values," Ensemble Theaters, accessed on April 28, 2018, https://www.ensembletheaters .net/about/values.
4. Michael Schneider, "Google Spent Two Years Studying 180 Teams. The Most Successful Ones Shared These 5 Traits," July 19, 2017, https://www.inc.com/michael-schneider/google -thought-they-knew-how-to-create-the-perfect.html.

Final Thoughts

1. William Hutchison Murray, *The Scottish Himalayan Expedition* (London: J.M. Dent & Sons, 1951), 6–7.

Appendix

1. Elin Spring, "'Character Study' @ deCordova," *What Will You Remember* (blog), May 1, 2013, http://elinspringphotography.com/blog/character-study-decordova/. Blog post references quote from exhibit text at the deCordova Museum in Lincoln, Massachusetts.

INDEX

ABOUT THE AUTHOR

 Driven by a passion to coach business leaders to develop their presence, tell compelling stories, and establish authentic connections, **Rob Salafia** combines two decades of experience as a top leadership development executive with a stellar past career in the performing arts. In his current professional role, he assists leaders in their quest to build sharper levels of emotional and narrative intelligence, transition into higher organizational levels, and share their vision and strategies in compelling and relevant ways.

When Rob was a performing artist, he traveled the globe delivering a unique, one-person variety show. At the heart of his approach to performance was the relationship he built with his audience, projecting a sense of warmth, confidence, and lightheartedness that permeates his work to this day. Now, as an executive coach, Rob takes great satisfaction in helping executives to emulate this type of performance in their leadership roles.

As a popular keynote speaker, Rob enjoys putting his skills to use, galvanizing audiences around critical learning and business topics at leadership conferences and company-organized events. Highlighted speaking engagements include events sponsored by Sony Music Entertainment, Johnson & Johnson, CREW Network, YPO/YPO Gold, ING Bank, MIT Sloan School of Management, Wharton Business School, Schulich School of Business, and the Association for Training and Development.

Rob is also a lecturer at MIT Sloan School of Management Executive Education Programs, and an MIT Leadership Center Master Executive Coach. He has cultivated a lasting partnership with Harvard Business School as well, resulting in the integration of experiential programming within the Harvard

MBA curriculum and Executive Education Leadership Programs serving thousands of global leaders.

As a learning partner and workshop facilitator, Rob has worked with Fortune 500 companies such as Digitas, Diageo, Sapient Consulting, NN Group, American Express, and Metro AG. He holds an MS in Organizational Policy from Boston University and a Graduate Certificate in Executive Coaching from William James College. For more info, visit his company website: http://protagonistconsulting.com/.

3 1333 04718 8196